Guide to
GERMAN
Idioms

Sprachführer zu
DEUTSCHEN
Idiomen

J.P. Lupson

PASSPORT BOOKS

Trade Imprint of National Textbook Company
Lincolnwood, Illinois U.S.A.

This edition first published in 1984 by Passport Books, Trade Imprint
of National Textbook Company, 4255 West Touhy Avenue,
Lincolnwood (Chicago), Illinois 60646-1975, which has been granted
exclusive publishing rights in North America and non-exclusive rights to
sell copies elsewhere. Originally published in the United Kingdom by
Stanley Thornes (Publishers) Ltd. ©1984 J.P. Lupson. All rights
reserved. No part of this book may be reproduced, stored in a
retrieval system, or transmitted in any form or by any means,
electronic, mechanical, recording or otherwise, without the prior
permission of National Textbook Company. Manufactured in the
U.S.A.

5 6 7 8 9 0 ML 9 8 7 6 5 4 3 2 1

Introduction

This book aims to provide a source of reference for all students of German, whether in schools, in institutions of Higher Education or in evening classes. It will also be of value to other Germanists who simply wish to enrich their knowledge of, and feel for, the German language.

Idioms can be a most rewarding aspect of language study, offering a fascinating glimpse into the forms of thought unique to a particular language community. It is this uniqueness that frequently makes it impossible to translate them literally. German idioms often contain a picture which has no discernible connection with their English meaning. For instance, one could hardly have guessed that the expression 'jemandem den Kopf waschen' (literally 'to wash someone's head') in fact means 'to give someone a piece of one's mind'. Nor could one have guessed that to say something 'durch die Blume' (literally 'through the flower') is to say something 'in a roundabout way', and that 'bei jemandem einen Stein im Brett haben' ('to have a stone in someone's board') means that one is 'well in' with someone. The German language contains many such expressions, and they constitute one of the sources of its richness and of its fascination.

Idioms tend to be used strategically; that is, they capture and express particular states of mind or particular observations of a speaker, at moments when maximum effect is desired with a minimum of language. An appreciation of their content and a sensitivity to their use in the correct context are, therefore, a mark of competent language use.

This book contains over 500 of the most commonly occurring idioms in the German language. They are of a kind that can be used without embarrassment in any social circle! However, in instances where a particular idiom is most likely to be encountered in informal conversation rather than, say, in a quality newspaper, it has been identified by the abbreviation 'coll.' (for colloquial). Other idioms, not specially marked, can be used in any context. It does not always follow that an informal German idiom has an informal English equivalent, or vice versa. For this reason the abbreviation 'coll.' has also been shown against the English translations, where their use is more restricted than that of the German idiom. Where appropriate, a distinction is made between British idioms (indicated with the abbreviation 'Br.') and American idioms ('Am.').

For easy reference the idioms in this book are presented in clearly defined subject areas and listed alphabetically within these areas. For each idiom, an example of its use is shown in a German sentence with an English translation. In instances where a literal translation of the German idiom bears little or no resemblance to the English meaning, a note on the origin of the German idiom has been added.

The book can be used in several ways:

(a) using the classified contents list, to discover appropriate idioms in a particular topic area;

(b) using the index of German key words, to track down the precise form of a particular half-remembered idiom;

(c) using the index of English idioms, to establish whether there is (or, in some cases, is not) an equivalent in German; and if so, whether it may be used in the same range of contexts as the English expression.

J.P.L.

Acknowledgements

I am grateful to a number of people for their interest and support in the preparation of this book. In particular I would like to thank Herbert Sasshofer, Ingrid Pagés and Gabriele Zagel for their careful scrutiny of the German text; Gillian Nuttall and Mandy Phillips for their helpful suggestions in portions of the English text; and Eileen Bird and Joan Mullinex for their assistance with reprographic work. My grateful thanks also to Elisabeth Daniel for typing the manuscript, and for her checking of the German text.

For Evelyn, Karen and Michael.

Auch für Oma, Tante Hedi, Onkel Franz
und Herbert, denen ich meine Liebe
zur deutschen Sprache verdanke.

Contents

SUBJECT AREAS

═══ 1. ANGER, ANNOYANCE, IRRITATION ═══

FUSS

mit dem linken Fuß zuerst aufgestanden sein (coll.)

to have got out of bed the wrong side (coll.)

Manfred ist heute überraschend brummig. Er ist wahrscheinlich mit dem linken Fuß zuerst aufgestanden.
Manfred is surprisingly grumpy today. He probably got out of bed the wrong side.

Origin: **It was an old superstition that the left-hand side of something was the unlucky side.**

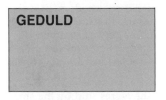

GEDULD

jemandem reißt die Geduld (coll.)

One's patience is wearing thin.

Mir reißt die Geduld. Hör doch endlich mit dem Geschrei auf!
My patience is wearing thin. Stop yelling!

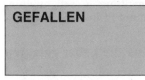

GEFALLEN

sich (dat.) etwas nicht gefallen lassen

not to put up with something

Dein schlechtes Benehmen lasse ich mir nicht gefallen.
I won't put up with your bad behaviour.

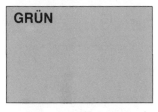

GRÜN

sich grün und blau ärgern (coll.)

to be extremely annoyed (with oneself)

Der Autor ärgerte sich grün und blau über die dummen Schreibfehler in seinem Manuskript.
The author was extremely annoyed at the silly spelling mistakes in his manuscript.

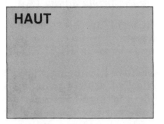

HAUT

Es ist zum Aus-der-Haut-Fahren. (coll.)

It's enough to drive you round the bend (coll.)/*up the wall.* (coll.)

Es ist zum Aus-der-Haut-Fahren, daß man sich diese ohrenbetäubende Musik ständig anhören muß.
It's enough to drive you round the bend to have to listen to this deafening music all the time.

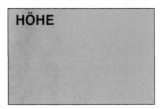

HÖHE

Das ist doch die Höhe!

That's just about the limit!

Das ist doch die Höhe! Du verschwendest dein ganzes Geld und dann fragst du, ob du mehr haben kannst.
That's just about the limit! You waste all your money and then you ask if you can have more.

1

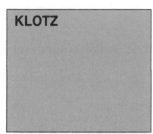

jemandem ein Klotz am Bein sein (coll.)

to be a millstone round someone's neck (coll.)

„Astrid ist mir ein Klotz am Bein", sagte Edith. „Wenn ich mit meinem Freund allein spazierengehen will, kommt sie immer mit!"
"Astrid is a millstone round my neck," said Edith. "Whenever I want to go for a walk alone with my boyfriend, she always comes with us!"

jemandem paßt etwas nicht in den Kram (coll.)

not to suit someone's plans at all

Daß wir nächste Woche nach Amerika auswandern, paßt meinem Sohn Thomas nicht in den Kram. Er hat eben eine neue Freundin kennengelernt, mit der er gern zusammen ist.
The fact that we are emigrating to America next week does not suit my son Thomas's plans at all. He has just met a new girlfriend whose company he enjoys.

Origin: **'Der Kram' referred to the wares sold by the small shopkeeper. He would be unwilling to sell anything outside of his line, i.e. that did not fit into his 'Kram'.**

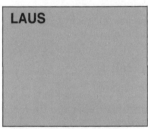

jemandem ist eine Laus über die Leber gelaufen

something is bugging someone (coll.), *something is eating someone* (coll.)

Ist dir eine Laus über die Leber gelaufen? Du bist heute so schlecht gelaunt.
Is something bugging you? You're in such a bad mood today.

Origin: **See 'Leberwurst' below.**

die beleidigte Leberwurst spielen (coll.)

to get in a huff (coll.), *to play the prima donna* (Am.)

Immer wenn sie ihren Willen nicht durchsetzen kann, spielt sie die beleidigte Leberwurst.
Whenever she can't get her own way she gets in a huff.

Origin: **The picture is of the sensitive liver being attacked by a louse, which has the effect of acutely irritating a person (c.f. the idiom 'jemandem ist eine Laus über die Leber gelaufen'). A person so affected acts 'die beleidigte Leberwurst', 'Wurst' being merely a humorous addition.**

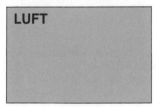

in die Luft gehen (coll.)

to go through the roof (coll.), *to blow one's top* (coll.)

Als mein Vater erfuhr, daß ich ihm nicht gehorcht hatte, ging er in die Luft.
When my father discovered that I had not obeyed him, he went through the roof.

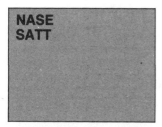

von etwas die Nase voll haben (coll.)
etwas satt haben (coll.)

to be fed up with something (coll.)*, to be sick of*
something (coll.)

Von seiner ständigen Frechheit habe ich die Nase
voll./Seine ständige Frechheit habe ich satt.
I'm fed up with/sick of his constant cheek.

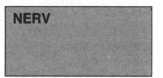

jemandem auf die Nerven gehen (coll.)

to get on someone's nerves (coll.)

Ihr ständiger Klatsch geht mir auf die Nerven.
Her constant gossiping gets on my nerves.

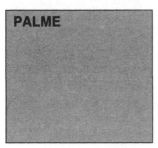

jemanden auf die Palme bringen (coll.)

to make someone's blood boil (coll.)*, to make someone see*
red (coll.)

Die ungerechte Behandlung gegenüber meinem Sohn
brachte mich auf die Palme.
The unfair treatment of my son made my blood boil.

Origin: **The picture is of an enraged monkey that swings**
up onto a palm-tree and chatters down angrily.

ein wunder Punkt
eine wunde Stelle

a sore point

Sag nichts von seiner Freundin. Das ist ein wunder
Punkt/eine wunde Stelle bei ihm: Sie haben letzte Woche
Krach gehabt und sind im Zorn auseinandergegangen.
Don't mention his girlfriend. It's a sore point: they had a row last
week and parted in anger.

jemandem geht etwas gegen den Strich

to go against the grain

Es geht mir gegen den Strich, mitten im Sommer heizen zu
müssen. Wann werden wir endlich warmes Wetter haben?
It goes against the grain having to put the heating on in the middle
of summer. When are we finally going to get warm weather?

Origin: **The comparison is with stroking a cat the wrong**
way, i.e. against the line of the fur's growth (gegen den
Strich).

2. APPEARANCE, DESCRIPTION

wie angegossen sitzen (coll.)

to fit like a glove, to be a perfect fit

Dieser Tirolerhut sitzt wie angegossen. Den kauf' ich als Andenken.
This Tyrolean hat is a perfect fit. I'll buy it as a souvenir.

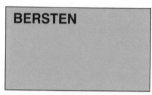

zum Bersten voll

full to bursting point

Beim Endspiel des Turniers war das Stadion zum Bersten voll.
In the final of the tournament the stadium was full to bursting point.

wie aus dem Ei gepellt

spick and span, spruce

In ihrer Sonntagskleidung sehen die Kinder aus wie aus dem Ei gepellt.
The children look spick and span in their Sunday best.

sich in Gala werfen

to get dressed up, to dress up

Für die Eröffnungszeremonie wird erwartet, daß man sich in Gala wirft.
One is expected to dress up for the opening ceremony.

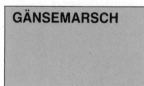

im Gänsemarsch gehen

to walk in single file

Die Touristen mußten im Gänsemarsch durch die enge Gasse gehen.
The tourists had to go in single file through the narrow street.

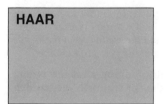

jemandem aufs Haar gleichen

to be the spitting image of someone (coll.)

Die Zwillinge gleichen sich aufs Haar. Ich kann sie nicht unterscheiden.
The twins are the spitting image of each other. I can't tell them apart.

gedrängt wie die Heringe (coll.)
gedrängt wie die Sardinen (coll.)
packed like sardines

Im Stadion standen wir gedrängt wie die Heringe/Sardinen.
In the stadium we stood packed like sardines.

wie Kraut und Rüben (coll.)
higgledy-piggledy (coll.), *all over the place* (coll.), *scattered*

Die Spielsachen liegen wie Kraut und Rüben auf dem Boden herum.
The toys are lying higgledy-piggledy on the floor.

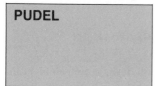

wie ein begossener Pudel dastehen
to look crestfallen, to look sorrowful

Als er seinen schlechten Aufsatz zurückbekam, stand er wie ein begossener Pudel da.
When he got back his bad essay he looked crestfallen.

3. APPROPRIATENESS, APTNESS, RELEVANCE

Kümmere dich nicht um ungelegte Eier. (prov.)
Don't cross your bridges until you come to them. (prov.)

Du machst dir unnötige Sorgen um Dinge, die wahrscheinlich nie passieren werden. Kümmere dich nicht um ungelegte Eier.
You worry needlessly about things that will probably never happen. Don't cross your bridges until you come to them.

Man soll das Fell des Bären nicht verteilen, bevor man ihn erlegt hat. (prov.)
Don't count your chickens before they're hatched. (prov.)

Nur weil du ein Vorstellungsgespräch hast, heißt das nicht, daß du die Stelle schon hast. Man soll das Fell des Bären nicht verteilen, bevor man ihn erlegt hat.
Just because you've got an interview it doesn't mean that you've already got the job. Don't count your chickens before they're hatched.

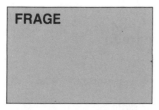

FRAGE

nicht in Frage kommen
to be out of the question

Johann möchte im Urlaub bergsteigen, aber das kommt nicht in Frage, weil ihm leicht schwindlig wird.
Johann would like to go mountain climbing on holiday but that is out of the question because he easily gets dizzy.

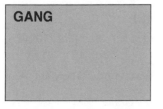

GANG

gang und gäbe sein
to be the custom

In Deutschland ist es gang und gäbe, Weihnachtsgeschenke am Heiligen Abend zu bekommen.
In Germany it is the custom to receive Christmas presents on Christmas Eve.

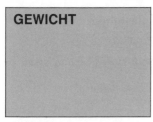

GEWICHT

nicht ins Gewicht fallen
to be of no consequence, to carry no weight

Friedl ist keine sehr gute Mutter. Was sie über die Erziehung von Kindern sagt, fällt deshalb einfach nicht ins Gewicht.
Friedl is not a very good mother. What she says about bringing children up, therefore, just doesn't carry any weight.

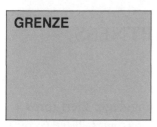

GRENZE

bei etwas die Grenze ziehen
to draw the line at something

Er wirkt als ein lässiger Kerl und nimmt an wenigen Sachen Anstoß. Bei Gewalttätigkeiten jeder Art aber zieht er die Grenze.
He comes across as an easy-going fellow and he takes offence at few things. However, he draws the line at violence of any kind.

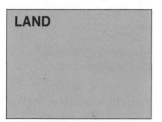

LAND

Andere Länder, andere Sitten. (prov.)
When in Rome, do as the Romans do. (prov.)

Wenn du nach England kommst, vergiß nicht, auf der linken Straßenseite zu fahren. Andere Länder, andere Sitten.
When you come to England don't forget to drive on the left-hand side of the road. When in Rome, do as the Romans do.

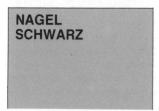

NAGEL
SCHWARZ

den Nagel auf den Kopf treffen
ins Schwarze treffen
to hit the nail on the head

Wenn du sagst, daß dieser Roman scheußlich ist, hast du den Nagel direkt auf den Kopf/direkt ins Schwarze getroffen!

You've hit the nail right on the head when you say this novel is awful!

Origin: **Schwarze: The reference is to the black bull's eye in the middle of the target in archery.**

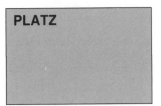

PLATZ

fehl am Platz sein

to be inappropriate/unsuitable

Bei der Abschlußfeier sind Jeans fehl am Platz. Du solltest deinen Anzug tragen.
Jeans are inappropriate for the graduation ceremony. You should wear your suit.

RECHT

zu seinem Recht kommen

to come into its own

Meine Kenntnisse in Erster Hilfe kamen beim Pfadfinderlager zu ihrem Recht. Zwei Kinder hatten kleine Schnittwunden und andere hatten Sportverletzungen.
My knowledge of first aid came into its own at the scout camp. Two children had small cuts and others had sports injuries.

SCHEMA

nach Schema F (coll.)

in a stereotyped way

Dieses Problem läßt sich nicht nach Schema F lösen. Man muß Initiative dazu aufbringen.
This problem can't be solved in a stereotyped way. It requires initiative.

Origin: **In the Prussian army reports from the Front were marked with the letter 'F'. There was a standard format for these reports, which was referred to as 'Schema F'.**

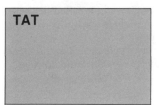

TAT

Die Tat wirkt mächtiger als das Wort. (prov.)

Actions speak louder than words. (prov.)

Tu endlich etwas, anstatt ständig Versprechungen zu machen! Die Tat wirkt mächtiger als das Wort.
You should do something instead of constantly making promises! Actions speak louder than words.

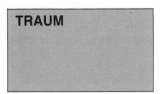

TRAUM

nicht im Traum daran denken

One wouldn't dream of it.

Ich denke nicht im Traum daran, mir einen so grauenhaften Film anzusehen.
I wouldn't dream of seeing such a gruesome film.

4. ATTITUDE, OUTLOOK

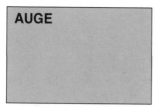

AUGE

ein Auge zudrücken

to turn a blind eye

Diesmal drücke ich ein Auge zu, aber wenn du das noch einmal machst, werde ich dich bestrafen.
This time I have turned a blind eye but if you do that again I shall punish you.

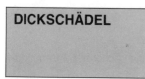

BRILLE

alles durch eine rosa(rote) Brille sehen

to see everything through rose-coloured glasses

Obgleich wir fast pleite sind, will mein Mann trotzdem einen teuren Urlaub in Acapulco buchen. Er sieht alles durch eine rosa(rote) Brille.
Although we're almost broke my husband still wants to book an expensive holiday in Acapulco. He sees everything through rose-coloured glasses.

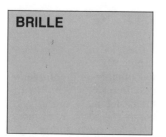

DICKSCHÄDEL

einen Dickschädel haben (coll.)

to be stubborn

Margit hat einen Dickschädel. Sie hört nie auf guten Rat.
Margit is stubborn. She never listens to good advice.

GEWICHT

großes Gewicht auf etwas (acc.) legen

to attach great importance to something, to set great store by something

Meine Tante Hedwig legt großes Gewicht auf Reinlichkeit. Schau, daß du dir die schmutzigen Schuhe tüchtig abwischst, bevor du ihr Haus betrittst.
My Aunt Hedwig sets great store by cleanliness. Make sure that you wipe your muddy feet properly before you go into her house.

GOLDWAAGE

nicht jedes Wort auf die Goldwaage legen

to take with a pinch of salt

Du sollst wegen gestern abend nicht beleidigt sein. Wenn die Hannelore jemanden neckt, darf man nicht jedes Wort auf die Goldwaage legen.
You shouldn't be offended because of yesterday evening. When Hannelore teases someone, you have to take what she says with a pinch of salt.

HERZ

mit halbem Herzen dabeisein
to be half-hearted about something

Diese Arbeit hat er schlecht gemacht, weil er nur mit halbem Herzen dabei war.
He did this work badly because he was only half-hearted about it.

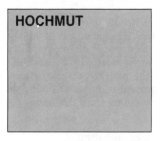

HOCHMUT

Hochmut kommt vor dem Fall. (prov.)
Pride goes before a fall. (prov.)

Der Oberbefehlshaber versuchte, die Regierung zu stürzen, aber der Putsch mißglückte, und alle seine Freunde verließen ihn. Hochmut kommt vor dem Fall.
The commander-in-chief tried to overthrow the government but the coup failed and all his friends abandoned him. Pride goes before a fall.

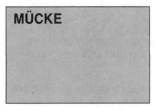

MÜCKE

aus einer Mücke einen Elefanten machen
to make a mountain out of a molehill

Sein Benehmen war gar nicht so anstößig, wie du behaupten willst. Mach doch aus einer Mücke keinen Elefanten.
His behaviour was nowhere near as offensive as you make out. Don't make a mountain out of a molehill.

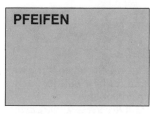

PFEIFEN

auf etwas (acc.) pfeifen (coll.)
to not care less about something (coll.), *to not care two hoots about something* (coll.)

Zu Monikas Party bin ich nicht eingeladen, aber ich pfeife eben darauf.
I haven't been invited to Monika's party but I couldn't care less.

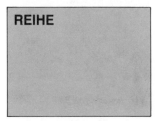

REIHE

aus der Reihe tanzen
to be different, to march to a different drummer (coll., Am.)

Er muß immer aus der Reihe tanzen. Egal was wir vorschlagen, er will das Gegenteil tun.
He has always got to be different. Whatever we suggest, he wants to do the opposite.

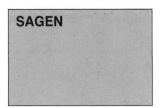

SAGEN

sich (dat.) von jemandem nichts sagen lassen
One won't be told anything.

Ich möchte ihm raten, was er machen sollte, aber er läßt sich von mir nichts sagen.
I would like to advise him about what he should do, but he won't be told.

SCHÄFCHEN

sein Schäfchen ins trockene bringen

to feather one's nest, to see oneself all right

Obwohl der Besitzer der Firma Bankrott gemacht hat, hat er sein Schäfchen ins trockene gebracht—er hatte nämlich ein Bankkonto in der Schweiz.
Although the owner of the company went bankrupt, he saw himself all right—you see, he had a bank account in Switzerland.

Origin: **Two possibilities: a) 'Schäfchen' derives from Low German 'schepken' = 'Schiffchen'. The picture is of a boat being taken on to dry land for the purpose of an overhaul, or for protection from an oncoming storm. b) 'Schäfchen' represents the possessions of the poorer person. Just as sheep are removed to higher ground in times of flood, so too does he try to save his possessions from the flood.**

SCHULTER

etwas auf die leichte Schulter nehmen

not to take something seriously enough

Wenn wir unser Pokalspiel gegen den Ortsverein auf die leichte Schulter nehmen, verlieren wir ganz bestimmt.
If we don't take our cup match against the local team seriously enough, we're bound to lose.

Origin: **It is not the shoulder as such that is meant here, but whether one considers something carried *on* the shoulder to be light or heavy.**

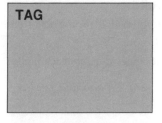

TAG

in den Tag hinein leben

to live for the moment

Du kannst nicht ewig in den Tag hinein leben. In zwei Wochen verläßt du die Schule, und du hast mit der Suche nach einer Stelle noch nicht einmal begonnen.
You can't always live for the moment. In two weeks you're leaving school and you haven't even started looking for a job.

TRÜBSAL

Trübsal blasen

to mope

Trübsal blasen ändert nichts an der Lage. Du mußt dich damit abfinden.
Moping won't alter the situation. You'll have to come to terms with it.

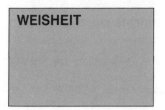

WEISHEIT

Man glaubt, die Weisheit mit Löffeln gegessen zu haben. (coll.)

to think one knows it.all (coll.)

Fritz glaubt, er hat die Weisheit mit Löffeln gegessen. Er läßt sich nichts sagen.
Fritz thinks he knows it all. He won't be told anything.

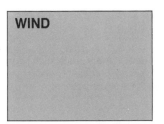

einen Rat in den Wind schlagen

to turn a deaf ear

Vor dem Unfall sagte ich ihm, was bei wildem Autofahren passieren könnte, aber er hat meinen Rat in den Wind geschlagen.
I told him before the accident what might happen if he drove recklessly, but he turned a deaf ear.

5. ATTRIBUTES OF CHARACTER, PERSONAL QUALITIES

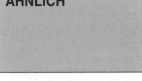

Das sieht ihm ganz ähnlich. (coll.)

That's just like him. (coll.)

Schon wieder hat er meinen Geburtstag vergessen. Das sieht ihm ganz ähnlich.
Once again he has forgotten my birthday. That's just like him.

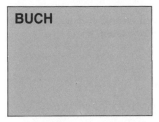

wie er (sie, es) im Buch steht

a textbook (or copybook, Br.) example

Eveline ist eine Mutter, wie sie im Buch steht. Sie ist verständnisvoll und geduldig und weiß auch mit ihren Kindern viel Spaß zu machen.
Eveline is a textbook example of a mother. She is understanding and patient and also knows how to have fun with her children.

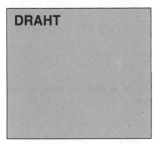

auf Draht sein (coll.)

to be on the ball (coll.), to know one's stuff (coll.)

Die Fluglotsen des verkehrsreichen O'Hare-Flughafens in Chicago müssen immer auf Draht sein, sonst könnte leicht ein Unglück passieren.
The air-traffic controllers at the busy O'Hare airport in Chicago have to be on the ball, otherwise an accident could easily happen.

Origin: **From an old expression meaning 'carefully sewn'.**

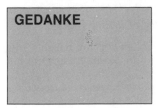

seine Gedanken beisammen haben

to have one's wits about one

Ich gehe heute früh ins Bett. Morgen bei der Fahrprüfung muß ich meine Gedanken beisammen haben.
I'm going to bed early tonight. I've got to have my wits about me in my driving test tomorrow.

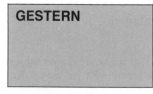

nicht von gestern sein (coll.)

not born yesterday (coll.)

Erzähl mir doch keine Geschichten! Ich bin doch nicht von gestern.
Don't try to tell me that! I wasn't born yesterday.

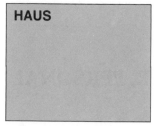

auf jemanden Häuser bauen können

to be able to rely on someone

Karla kommt bestimmt. Auf die kann man Häuser bauen.
Karla is sure to come. You can rely on her.

Origin: **The picture here is of someone being as dependable as the solid rock on which one builds a house. (Note: the idiom is often used omitting 'Häuser').**

Bei ihm ist Hopfen und Malz verloren. (coll.)

He's a dead loss. (coll.) *He's hopeless.* (coll.)

Mein Vetter kommt nie pünktlich. Wenn er sagt, er trifft mich um ein Uhr, kommt er bestimmt erst um zwei. Bei ihm ist Hopfen und Malz verloren.
My cousin is never punctual. If he says he'll meet me at one, he's bound not to arrive until two. He's a dead loss.

Origin: **If beer had been brewed wrongly, it was said that the hops and the malt had been wasted.**

vor die Hunde gehen
unter die Räder kommen

to go to the dogs (coll.), *to go to rack and ruin*

In den letzten paar Jahren ist Hans vor die Hunde gegangen/unter die Räder gekommen. Er ist jetzt rauschgiftsüchtig und bekommt immer Schwierigkeiten mit der Polizei.
In the past few years Hans has gone to the dogs. He's now a drug addict and is always in trouble with the police.

Origin: **Hunde: The picture here is of sick or weak game being easy prey for hunting dogs.**

Er kocht auch nur mit Wasser.

He's no different from anyone else/He puts his pants on just like everyone else, one leg at a time (Am.).

Du solltest doch keine Hemmungen vor ihm haben. Trotz seines Ruhms und seines Reichtums kocht er auch nur mit Wasser.
You shouldn't be shy of him. In spite of his fame and wealth he's no different from anyone else.

The boxes at left are labelled:

GESTERN

HAUS

HOPFEN

HUND
RAD

KOCHEN

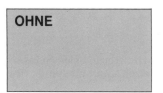

nicht ohne sein (coll.)

to have what it takes (coll.)

Amanda wird im Leben viel Erfolg haben. Sie ist nicht ohne.
Amanda will have much success in life. She's got what it takes.

jemanden in den Sack stecken
jemanden in die Tasche stecken

to put someone in the shade

Mit ihm will ich nicht mehr konkurrieren. Er steckt mich immer in den Sack/die Tasche.
I don't want to compete with him any more. He always puts me in the shade.

Origin: **From medieval wrestling. The winner of the contest would put his defeated opponent into a sack for the merriment of the spectators. (The idiom is also used with 'Tasche', this being the modern term for 'Hosensack'.)**

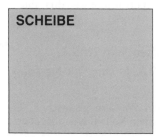

sich (dat.) von jemandem eine Scheibe abschneiden (coll.)

to take a leaf out of someone's book

Von der Tante Hedi können sich viele eine Scheibe abschneiden. Auch wenn sie unter Druck ist, bleibt sie geduldig und freundlich.
Many people can take a leaf out of Aunt Hedi's book. Even when she is under pressure she remains patient and friendly.

kein Sitzfleisch haben (coll.)

to have no staying power (coll.)

Das Erlernen einer Fremdsprache macht Spaß, ist jedoch auch anstrengend und zeitraubend. Wer kein Sitzfleisch hat, schafft es nicht.
Learning a foreign language is fun but it is also demanding and time-consuming. A person who has no staying power won't succeed in it.

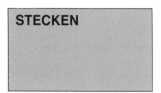

zeigen, was in einem steckt (coll.)

to show what one is made of

Unter schwierigen Umständen zeigt man, was in einem steckt.
In difficult circumstances people show what they are made of.

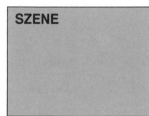

sich in Szene setzen

to play to the gallery

Sie ist ein Mensch, der nicht im Hintergrund bleiben kann. Sie muß sich immer in Szene setzen und Mittelpunkt des Interesses sein.
She is a person who cannot remain in the background. She always has to play to the gallery and be the centre of interest.

jemandem das Wasser nicht reichen können

not to be able to hold a candle to someone, not to be in the same league as someone (coll.)

Du bist ein gekonnter Tennisspieler, aber dem Kurt kannst du das Wasser nicht reichen. Er bringt es ohne Zweifel sehr weit in diesem Sport.
You're a competent tennis player but you're not in the same league as Kurt. Without doubt he is going to go far in this sport.

Origin: **Prior to the time when forks were used to eat meals, the nobility were served a bowl of water with which to wash their hands. This duty was performed by a page on bended knee. The idiom originally meant that one was considered unworthy to perform even this most menial of duties.**

mit allen Wassern gewaschen sein (coll.)

to be a smooth customer (coll.), *to know all the tricks* (coll.)

Jener Autohändler ist mit allen Wassern gewaschen. Er könnte einen Schubkarren für einen Rolls-Royce ausgeben.
That car dealer is a smooth customer. He could pass off a wheelbarrow as a Rolls Royce.

Origin: **From the idea of a widely travelled sailor who has swum and washed in all the oceans of the world.**

6. BOREDOM

Daumen drehen (coll.)

to twiddle one's thumbs

Wenn du dauernd Daumen drehst, wird der Brief nie fertig.
If you just sit there twiddling your thumbs the letter will never get finished.

EINSCHLAFEN	**Es ist zum Einschlafen. (coll.)** *It's enough to put (or send Br.) you to sleep.* Dieser Film ist furchtbar langweilig. Es ist zum Einschlafen. *This film is terribly boring. It's enough to put you to sleep.*
TOD	**sich zu Tode langweilen** *to bore someone to death* Seine blöden Witze langweilen mich zu Tode. *His stupid jokes bore me to death.*

7. BUSYNESS, OVERWORK, PREOCCUPATION

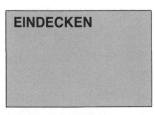

EINDECKEN · **mit Arbeit eingedeckt sein**
to have one's work cut out, to be snowed under with work

Ich kann leider nicht mitkommen. Ich bin mit Arbeit eingedeckt.
Unfortunately I can't come with you. I'm snowed under with work.

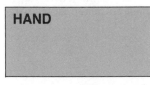

HAND · **alle Hände voll zu tun haben**
to have one's hands full

Wir ziehen heute um, da haben wir alle Hände voll zu tun.
We're moving house today so we've got our hands full.

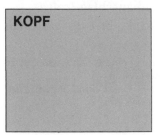

KOPF · **Mir raucht der Kopf.**
My head is spinning.

Diese Übersetzung ist furchtbar schwierig. Die meisten Vokabeln kenne ich nicht, und es sind auch unheimlich viele Nebensätze. Mir raucht der Kopf.
This translation is terribly difficult. I don't know most of the vocabulary and there is also an incredible number of subordinate clauses. My head is spinning.

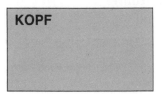

KOPF · **nicht wissen, wo einem der Kopf steht (coll.)**
not to know whether one is coming or going (coll.)

Ich habe so viel zu tun, ich weiß nicht, wo mir der Kopf steht.
I've so much to do I don't know whether I'm coming or going.

KOPF

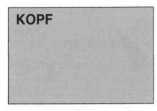

den Kopf voll haben

to have a lot on one's mind

Der Chef hat den Kopf voll. Er muß heute viele un-
angenehme Entscheidungen treffen.
*The boss has a lot on his mind. He has got to make a lot of
unpleasant decisions today.*

LUFT

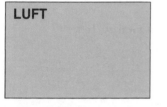

kaum Zeit haben, Luft zu holen

to have hardly time to breathe

Sie hat derzeit so viel Arbeit, daß sie kaum Zeit hat, Luft zu
holen.
*She has so much work at present that she has hardly time to
breathe.*

OHR

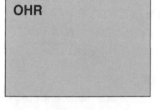

viel um die Ohren haben (coll.)

to be rushed off one's feet (coll.), *to be up to one's ears in
work, to have a lot on one's plate* (coll., Br.)

Leider kann ich heute nicht mitkommen. Ich habe viel um
die Ohren.
I'm afraid I can't come with you today. I'm rushed off my feet.

SCHINDEREI

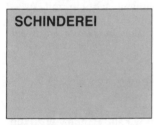

eine arge Schinderei (coll.)

a slog (coll., Br.), *a grind* (coll., Am.)

Ich wünschte, ich hätte ein Auto, denn jeden Tag 20
Kilometer mit dem Rad zur Arbeit zu fahren ist eine arge
Schinderei.
*I wish I had a car because travelling 12 miles to work by bike every
day is a real slog/a real grind.*

TAUBENSCHLAG

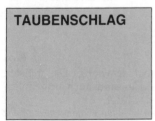

zugehen wie in einem Taubenschlag (coll.)

It's like Piccadilly Circus. (coll., Br.) *It's like Grand
Central Station.* (coll., Am.)

In unserem Haus geht es zu wie in einem Taubenschlag. Es
ist ein ständiges Kommen und Gehen.
*Our house is like Piccadilly Circus/Grand Central Station. There
are people coming and going the whole time.*

TRAB

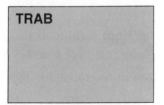

jemanden in Trab halten (coll.)

to keep someone on the go (coll.)

Unser kleiner Sohn Michael ist ein sehr aktives Kind. Er
hält uns ständig in Trab.
*Our little son Michael is a very active child. He constantly keeps
us on the go.*

ZEUG

sich ins Zeug legen

to work flat out, to go hammer and tongs at something

Wenn du die vielen Briefe heute noch fertigschreiben willst, mußt du dich ins Zeug legen.
If you want to get all those letters written by today you'll have to work flat out.

Origin: **'Zeug' here refers to the harness of the draught animal.**

8. CENSURE, REPROOF

DRAN

dran sein (coll.)

I) to be for the high jump (coll.)
II) to be someone's turn*

I) Dein Konto ist schon wieder ohne Erlaubnis weit über-zogen? Jetzt bist du aber wirklich dran.
Your account is heavily overdrawn yet again? Now you're really for the high jump.

II) Heute bin ich mit dem Abwaschen dran.
Today it's my turn to do the washing-up.

* Although this meaning does not fit into the category of 'Censure, Reproof' it has been included for interest.

**FEDERLESEN
PROZESS**

**nicht viel Federlesens mit jemandem machen
kurzen Prozeß mit jemandem machen**

to give someone short shrift, to waste no time on someone

Die Hausfrau machte nicht viel Federlesens/machte kurzen Prozeß mit dem Vertreter. Er war schon der vierte an jenem Morgen, der bei ihr geklingelt hatte.
The housewife wasted no time on the salesman. He was the fourth one already that morning who had rung at her door.

Origin: **Federlesen: To ingratiate oneself with people of standing, a person at one time might pick off (lesen) any feather (Feder) that had landed on their clothing. Such a person was known as a 'Federleser', i.e. a 'creep'.**

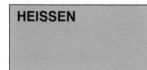

HEISSEN

Was soll das heißen? (coll.)

What's the meaning of this?

Was soll das heißen? Warum bist du nicht in der Schule?
What's the meaning of this? Why aren't you in school?

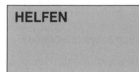

Ich werde dir helfen! (coll.)

I'll give you what for! (coll.)

Wenn ich dich wieder fluchen höre, werde ich dir helfen!
If I hear you swearing again I'll give you what for!

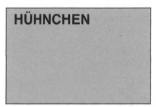

ein Hühnchen mit jemandem zu rupfen haben

to have a bone to pick with someone

Ich habe mit ihm ein Hühnchen zu rupfen. Er hat Unwahrheiten über mich verbreitet.
I have a bone to pick with him. He has spread false rumours about me.

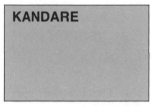

jemanden an die Kandare nehmen

to take a hard line with someone

Unseren Neffen muß man an die Kandare nehmen. Er ist frech und faul.
You have to take a hard line with our nephew. He is cheeky and lazy.

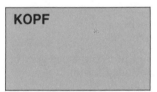

und wenn du dich auf den Kopf stellst (coll.)

no matter what you do/say

Du gehst morgen nicht mit, und wenn du dich auf den Kopf stellst.
You're not going with them tomorrow, no matter what you say.

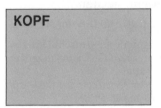

jemandem den Kopf waschen (coll.)

to give someone a piece of one's mind

Dafür, daß er so spät in der Nacht nach Hause gekommen ist, hat ihm seine Mutter den Kopf gewaschen.
His mother gave him a piece of her mind for coming home so late at night.

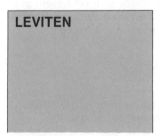

jemandem die Leviten lesen

to tell someone where to get off (coll.), to read someone the riot act (coll.)

Den Kindern, die in seinem Garten Äpfel gestohlen hatten, hat Elkes Onkel die Leviten gelesen.
Elke's uncle told the children who had been stealing apples in his garden where to get off.

Origin: **The book of Leviticus in the Old Testament was written for the instruction of the Levite priests (die Leviten). The idiom developed more than 1200 years ago when portions of the book were read by Bishop Chrodegang of Metz to some of his clergy in order to rebuke them for their wayward behaviour.**

MARSCH

jemandem den Marsch blasen (coll.)

to give someone what for (coll.), *to give someone a rocket* (coll., Br.)

Nachdem mein Vater mein schlechtes Zeugnis gelesen hatte, hat er mir den Marsch geblasen.
When my father had read my bad report he really gave me what for.

Origin: **A military derivation from the custom of the march-off or the advance being sounded by the regimental musicians (buglers, etc.).**

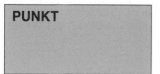

OHR

sich (dat.) etwas hinter die Ohren schreiben (coll.)

to get something into one's thick head (coll.)

Schon wieder hast du den Zug versäumt! Schreib es dir hinter die Ohren, daß er täglich um Punkt acht Uhr abfährt.
You've missed the train again! Get it into your thick head that it leaves every day at 8 o'clock sharp.

Origin: **It was once the practice that when boundary stones were being laid or important contracts signed, boys were present to act as witnesses for the next generation should any dispute arise. To ensure that the boys recalled the particular event, they were given a slap round the ear to reinforce their memory. This was referred to as 'writing the event behind their ears'.**

PUNKT

Jetzt mach mal einen Punkt! (coll.)

Come off it! (coll.)

Jetzt mach mal einen Punkt! Das hat er gar nicht gesagt.
Come off it! He didn't say that at all.

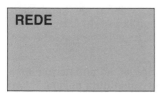

REDE

jemanden zur Rede stellen

to take someone to task

Weil Kathrin immer zu spät zur Arbeit kam, hat ihre Chefin sie zur Rede gestellt.
Kathrin's boss took her to task for always coming to work late.

SAITE

andere Saiten aufziehen (coll.)

to take a harder line, to get tough (coll.)

Der Gefreite kam selten rechtzeitig zum Dienst. Daher hat der Kommandant andere Saiten aufgezogen und ihm den Ausgang gesperrt.
The lance-corporal (USA: private, first class) rarely arrived on duty on time, so the commanding officer got tough, and confined him to barracks.

Origin: **'Saiten auf ein Instrument aufziehen' means 'to string an instrument'. The picture in this idiom, therefore, is that of putting a different set of strings on an instrument; by extension, trying a different approach.**

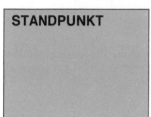

STANDPUNKT

jemandem seinen Standpunkt klarmachen

to make one's feelings/position clear to someone

Herbert wollte den neuen Computer kaufen, aber ich habe ihm tüchtig meinen Standpunkt klargemacht. Der kostet einfach zu viel.
Herbert wanted to buy the new computer but I made my position perfectly clear to him. It simply costs too much.

9. CERTAINTY, CONVICTION

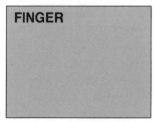

FINGER

sich (dat.) etwas an den fünf Fingern abzählen

It's as clear as daylight. It sticks out a mile. (coll.) *It's as plain as the nose on your face.*

Daß die Freundin des Chefs die Beförderung bekommt, kann man sich an den fünf Fingern abzählen.
It's as clear as daylight that the boss's girlfriend will get the promotion.

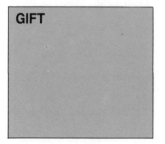

GIFT

Darauf kannst du Gift nehmen. (coll.)

You can bet your life on it. (coll.)

Wenn sie nach Wien kommen, werden sie mindestens einmal in die Oper gehen. Darauf kannst du Gift nehmen.
When they come to Vienna they will go to the opera at least once. You can bet your life on it.

Origin: **From a medical practice of administering to a patient a non-harmful medicine containing poison.**

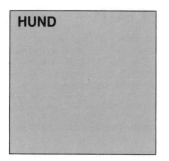

Da liegt der Hund begraben.

That's the crux of the matter. That's at the root of it.

Du spielst so schlecht Klavier, nicht weil du wenig Talent hast, sondern weil du nicht genug übst. Da liegt der Hund begraben.
You play the piano so badly, not because you have little talent, but because you don't practise enough. That's the crux of the matter.

Origin: **Nothing to do with dogs. 'Die hunde' was Middle High German for 'treasure'.**

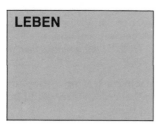

aus dem Leben gegriffen

taken from real life

Manche Beispielsätze in jenem Buch von französischen Redewendungen sind unmittelbar aus dem Leben gegriffen.
Many example sentences in that book of French idioms are taken directly from real life.

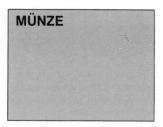

etwas für bare Münze nehmen

to take something at face value, to take something for real

Die Versprechungen von Politikern vor den Wahlen nehmen viele Leute nicht für bare Münze.
Many people do not take the promises of politicians before elections for real.

Stein und Bein schwören

to swear blind (coll.)

Der Bankangestellte hat Stein und Bein geschworen, daß er das Geld nicht gestohlen hatte, aber die Polizei hat es ihm doch nachweisen können.
The bank clerk swore blind that he hadn't stolen the money but nevertheless the police were able to prove that he had.

Origin: **When swearing an oath before witnesses it was at one time the practice to touch the altar stone (Stein) of the shrine of a saint containing his/her 'Gebeine' (Bein), i.e. his/her bones.**

10. CONVERSATION, SPEECH

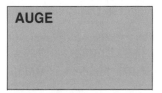

AUGE

mit jemandem unter vier Augen sprechen

to talk privately with someone

Darf ich mit Ihnen unter vier Augen sprechen? Ich habe ein Problem.
May I talk to you privately? I have a problem.

BLATT

kein Blatt vor den Mund nehmen

not to mince one's words

Der Klempner nahm kein Blatt vor den Mund. Er sagte dem Lehrling, er sei faul und seine Arbeit sei schlampig.
The plumber didn't mince his words. He told the apprentice that he was lazy and that his work was sloppy.

Origin: **From the practice of placing a leaf or a sheet of paper in front of one's mouth so that one's voice would be muffled when telling unpleasant things.**

BLUME

etwas durch die Blume sagen

to say something in a roundabout way

Sie ist ein empfindlicher Typ. Sag ihr lieber durch die Blume, daß ihr die Frisur nicht steht.
She is a sensitive type. It would be better to tell her in a roundabout way that the hairstyle doesn't suit her.

Origin: **Flowers have traditionally been a way of expressing one's feelings. Thus, by implication, to express something unpleasant by means of flowers is to take the sting out of it.**

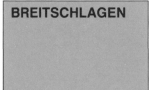

BREITSCHLAGEN

jemanden breitschlagen (coll.)

to talk someone round (coll.)

Erika will nicht mit uns zum Schwimmen kommen, aber ich werde sie noch breitschlagen.
Erika doesn't want to come swimming with us but I'll talk her round yet.

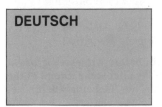

DEUTSCH

auf gut deutsch

in plain language, putting it plainly

Du hast in den Automaten eine ausländische Münze eingeworfen? Auf gut deutsch nennt man das Unehrlichkeit.
You put a foreign coin in the machine? Putting it plainly that's called dishonesty.

ein heißes Eisen

a hot potato (coll.), *a tricky subject* (coll.)

Bei einem Konjunkturrückgang ist Arbeitslosigkeit in der Tagespolitik immer ein heißes Eisen.
At a time of economic recession, unemployment is always a hot potato in the politics of the day.

Origin: **As a medieval form of trial, the accused had to carry a hot iron for a certain distance. If it did not burn him, he was found innocent.**

den Faden verlieren

to lose the thread

Der Redner stockte mitten in seiner Rede. Er hatte den Faden verloren und konnte seine Argumentation nicht entwickeln.
The speaker faltered in the middle of his speech. He had lost the thread and couldn't develop his line of argument.

Origin: **From a Greek legend. Ariadne gave her lover Theseus a ball of thread to enable him to find his way out of the labyrinth.**

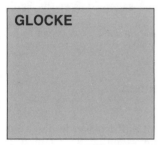

etwas an die große Glocke hängen

to bandy something about (coll.), *to broadcast something*

Daß er ein Toupet hat, sollst du nicht an die große Glocke hängen. Er will nicht, daß andere von seiner Glatze wissen.
Don't bandy it about that he's got a toupee. He doesn't want anyone to know he's bald.

Origin: **From the practice of ringing church bells to proclaim important news.**

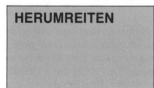

auf etwas (dat.) herumreiten (coll.)

to keep on about something (coll.)

Mit ihnen rede ich nicht gern. Sie reiten immer auf dem gleichen alten Thema herum.
I don't like talking to them. They keep on about the same old thing.

HERZ

jemandem sein Herz ausschütten

to pour one's heart out to someone

Sie war den Tränen nahe und schüttete mir ihr Herz aus.
She was close to tears and poured her heart out to me.

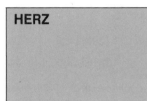

HERZ

sich (dat.) etwas vom Herzen reden

to get something off one's chest

Er hat mich gestern furchtbar geärgert. Ich muß dir davon erzählen, um es mir vom Herzen zu reden.
He really annoyed me yesterday. I must tell you about it to get it off my chest.

HUNDERT

vom Hundertsten ins Tausendste kommen

to get carried away, to ramble on

Diesen Redner mag ich nicht. Er kommt vom Hundertsten ins Tausendste und berührt kaum das eigentliche Thema.
I don't like this speaker. He gets carried away and barely touches on the matter in hand.

Origin: **An unsophisticated calculating implement (abacus) in use from the 15th to the 17th century. One could quite easily transpose, by error, 100 to 1000.**

KATZE

wie die Katze um den heißen Brei herumgehen/herumschleichen

to beat about (Am. around) the bush

Du kannst nicht wie die Katze um den heißen Brei herumschleichen. Du mußt ihm direkt sagen, daß er die Stelle nicht bekommen hat.
You can't beat about (Am. around) the bush. You've got to tell him straight that he hasn't got the job.

KIND

das Kind beim Namen nennen

to call a spade a spade

Da hört doch die Gemütlichkeit auf! Ich werde das Kind beim Namen nennen und ihm sagen, daß er faul und unzuverlässig ist.
That's the limit! I'm going to call a spade a spade and tell him that he's unreliable and lazy.

Origin: **From the practice of pretending that one's illegitimate child was one's nephew or niece so as to avoid embarrassment. In full, this idiom reads 'das Kind beim rechten Namen nennen', i.e. to come clean about a child's real identity and admit that he/she is illegitimate.**

KURZ

kurz und gut

in a nutshell, in short, in a word

Diesen Sommer kann ich nicht ins Ausland reisen. Kurz und gut, ich bin pleite.
I can't go abroad this summer. In a word, I'm broke.

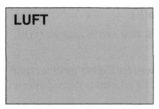

LUFT

seinem Herzen Luft machen (coll.)
to give vent to one's feelings

Ich werde meinem Herzen Luft machen und ihm sagen, daß ich mit seinem Benehmen völlig unzufrieden bin.
I'm going to give vent to my feelings and tell him that I am completely dissatisfied with his behaviour.

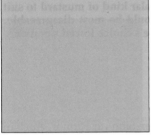
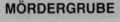

MÖRDERGRUBE

aus seinem Herzen keine Mördergrube machen
to make no bones about it

Sie machte aus ihrem Herzen keine Mördergrube und sagte dem Abteilungsleiter, daß er keine Ahnung von Organisation hätte.
She made no bones about it and told the head of department that he had no idea about organisation.

Origin: **From Luther's translation of Matthew 21:13 — 'Mein Haus soll ein Bethaus heißen; ihr aber habt eine Mördergrube daraus gemacht.'**

MUND

nicht auf den Mund gefallen sein (coll.)
to have the gift of the gab (coll.)

Er kann sich aus allen Schwierigkeiten herausreden. Kein Wunder — er ist nicht auf den Mund gefallen.
He can talk himself out of all difficulties. No wonder — he has the gift of the gab.

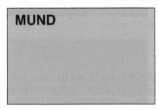

MUND

jemandem nach dem Mund reden
to say what someone wants to hear

Um im Berufsleben weiterzukommen, redet Heinrich dem Chef immer nach dem Mund.
To get on in his career Heinrich always says what the boss wants to hear.

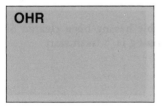

OHR

jemandem mit etwas in den Ohren liegen
to go on at someone about something

Immer wenn wir einkaufen gehen, liegt mir meine Tochter in den Ohren, daß sie ein neues Fahrrad will.
Whenever we go shopping my daughter goes on at me about wanting a new bicycle.

OHR

ganz Ohr sein
to be all ears

Erzähl mir, was dir passiert ist. Ich bin ganz Ohr.
Tell me what happened to you. I'm all ears.

When I mentioned the name of their favourite singer, the two girls pricked up their ears.

Origin: **The picture is of animals such as the dog and the horse whose ears straighten when they are attentive or on the alert.**

13. DECEPTION, FALSENESS

blinder Alarm

a false alarm

Als ich über Lautsprecher hörte, daß der letzte Zug gestrichen worden war, war ich entsetzt. Aber es war nur blinder Alarm — das sollte erst ab nächste Woche in Kraft treten.
When I heard over the loudspeakers that the last train had been cancelled I was horrified. However, it was just a false alarm — it was only to come into effect from next week.

Das steht auf einem anderen Blatt.

That's a different kettle of fish. (coll.) That's a different story.

Vor der Öffentlichkeit wirkt jener Politiker verständnisvoll und gütig, aber wie er sich in der Familie benimmt, das steht auf einem anderen Blatt.
In public that politician comes across as understanding and kind, but his behaviour at home is a different story.

jemanden auf die falsche Fährte bringen

to put someone on the wrong track

Irgend jemand hat der Polizei eine irreführende Auskunft gegeben und sie dadurch bei der Suche nach dem Verbrecher auf die falsche Fährte gebracht.
Someone gave the police a misleading piece of information, and in doing so put them on the wrong track in their search for the criminal.

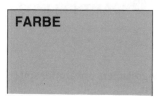

jemanden zwingen, Farbe zu bekennen

to call someone's bluff

Ich glaube Heinz nicht, wenn er sagt, daß er fließend Italienisch spricht. Zwingen wir ihn, Farbe zu bekennen. Du, Mario, bist Italiener. Red es mal mit ihm.

I don't believe Heinz when he says he speaks fluent Italian. Let's call his bluff. Mario, you're Italian. Talk to him in it.

Origin: **From cards. 'Farbe bekennen' means 'to follow suit'.**

FEDER

sich mit fremden Federn schmücken

to claim all the glory, to deck oneself out in borrowed plumes (dated)

Eigentlich hat nicht der Professor sondern sein Student diese große Entdeckung gemacht. Jener schmückt sich mit fremden Federn.
Actually it wasn't the professor but his student who made this great discovery. The former is claiming all the glory.

Origin: **From the fable 'The Crow and the Peacock' (by the Roman Phaedrus) in which the former decked itself out in the plumes of the latter.**

FELL

jemandem das Fell über die Ohren ziehen (coll.)

to pull the wool over someone's eyes

Den Händler hielt ich für ehrlich, aber er hat mir gehörig das Fell über die Ohren gezogen. Das Auto, das er mir verkauft hat, ist ein richtiger Klapperkasten.
I thought the dealer was honest but he properly pulled the wool over my eyes. The car he sold me is a real heap.

Origin: **From the practice of the knacker who pulled the animal's skin off over its head after the ears had been removed. A parallel expression in English is to 'fleece' someone.**

FRIEDEN

Ich traue dem Frieden nicht.

It's too good to last.

Almut und Bernd spielen heute einträchtig miteinander, obwohl sie sich normalerweise ständig zanken. Ich traue dem Frieden nicht.
Almut and Bernd are playing peaceably together today although they normally always quarrel. It's too good to last.

Origin: **In the Middle Ages, German Emperors decreed from time to time that peace was to be observed between various subject states which were at war. However, as the imperial army was unable to enforce the decrees, 'peace' became a very hollow term.**

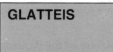

GLATTEIS

jemanden aufs Glatteis führen

to lead someone up the garden path (coll.), *to take someone for a ride* (coll.)

14. DESPAIR

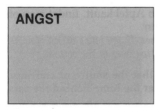

in tausend Ängsten schweben

to be frantic

Wir schwebten in tausend Ängsten, als es Mitternacht schlug und Elke noch immer nicht zu Hause war.
We were frantic when midnight struck and Elke still hadn't returned.

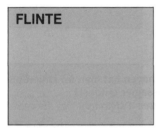

die Flinte ins Korn werfen

to throw in the towel, to give up

Wirf nicht die Flinte ins Korn! Hilfe kommt schon.
Don't give up! Help is on its way.

Origin: **A soldier running after defeat in battle might throw his gun away (e.g. into a cornfield) so as to be able to run faster.**

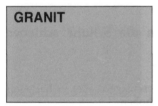

auf Granit beißen (coll.)

to bang one's head against a brick wall (coll.)

Frag deinen Vater nicht, ob du mitkommen kannst. Du beißt auf Granit — er sagt bestimmt wieder nein.
Don't ask your father if you can come with us. You'll be banging your head against a brick wall — he's bound to say "No!" again.

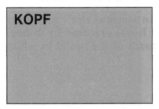

den Kopf verlieren

to lose one's head

Als es im Wald dunkel wurde, verlor Lisbeth den Kopf und fing zu schreien an.
As it got dark in the wood, Lisbeth lost her head and she began to scream.

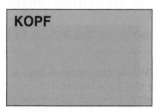

die Hände über dem Kopf zusammenschlagen

to throw up one's hands in horror

Als Margit erfuhr, daß sie die Prüfung nicht bestanden hatte, schlug sie die Hände über dem Kopf zusammen.
When Margit discovered that she had failed the exam, she threw up her hands in horror.

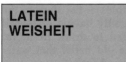

mit seinem Latein am Ende sein
mit seiner Weisheit am Ende sein

to be at one's wits' end

Ich habe kein Geld mehr, und morgen muß ich die Miete bezahlen. Ich bin mit meinem Latein am Ende.
I have no money and tomorrow I have to pay the rent. I'm at my wits' end.

Origin: **Latein: A reference to the pupil learning Latin who faltered in the middle of a Latin speech because of a lack of vocabulary.**

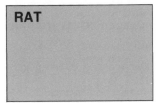

RAT

Nun ist guter Rat teuer.
It's hard to know what to do. What is one to do now?

Der letzte Zug ist schon weg, und ich habe kein Fahrgeld für den Bus. Nun ist guter Rat teuer.
The last train has already gone and I've no bus fare. What am I going to do now?

15. DETERMINATION, PERSISTENCE

APFEL
PILLE

in den sauren Apfel beißen
die bittere Pille schlucken

to grasp the nettle (Br.), *to bite the bullet* (now rare in Br.)

Ich möchte lieber in der Sonne liegen, aber das schmutzige Geschirr steht meterhoch in der Küche. Ich werde in den sauren Apfel beißen/Ich werde die bittere Pille schlucken und es abwaschen.
I would rather lie in the sun but the dirty dishes are piled up in the kitchen. I'll grasp the nettle and wash them up.

BIEGEN

auf Biegen oder Brechen
come what may, whatever it takes, by hook or by crook

Hans will auf Biegen oder Brechen das Spiel gewinnen.
Hans wants to win the game, whatever it takes.

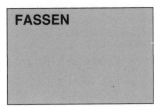

FASSEN

sich auf etwas gefaßt machen
to prepare oneself for something

Der Chef will dich sprechen. Mach dich auf eine schlechte Nachricht gefaßt.
The boss wants to speak to you. Prepare yourself for some bad news.

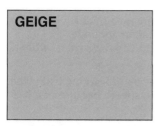

die erste Geige spielen

to call the tune

Obgleich der Präsident ein angesehener und beliebter Mensch ist, weiß jeder, daß der Befehlshaber der Armee die erste Geige spielt.
Although the President is a respected and popular man, everyone knows that the commander of the army calls the tune.

sich mit Händen und Füßen gegen etwas wehren

to fight something tooth and nail

Die Gewerkschaft hat sich mit Händen und Füßen gegen die Stillegung der Fabrik gewehrt.
The union fought the closure of the factory tooth and nail.

alle Hebel in Bewegung setzen

to leave no stone unturned

Die Polizei setzte alle Hebel in Bewegung, um den Massenmörder zu fassen.
The police left no stone unturned in the hunt for the mass murderer.

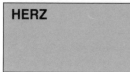

sich (dat.) ein Herz fassen

to pluck up courage

Ich konnte mir zum Springen kein Herz fassen.
I couldn't pluck up courage to jump.

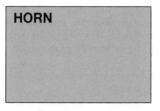

den Stier bei den Hörnern packen

to take the bull by the horns

Pamela war nie im Leben Ski gefahren, aber sie packte den Stier bei den Hörnern und fuhr die Piste hinunter.
Pamela had never skied in her life but she took the bull by the horns and went down the slope.

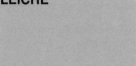

über Leichen gehen (coll.)

to stop at nothing (coll.)

Er würde über Leichen gehen, um sich im Beruf emporzuarbeiten.
He would stop at nothing to get on in his career.

gute Miene zum bösen Spiel machen

to put up a brave front, to put on a brave face (Br.)

Obgleich er für die Nationalmannschaft nicht aufgestellt worden ist, macht er gute Miene zum bösen Spiel.

Although he hasn't been picked for the national team, he's putting up a brave front.

Origin: **From cards. The player with a bad hand must not betray the fact with his facial expression.**

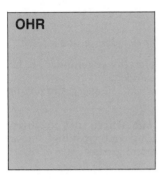

die Ohren steifhalten (coll.)

to keep a stiff upper lip

„Morgen muß ich zum Zahnarzt gehen. Ich fürchte mich."
„Halt nur die Ohren steif. Es ist nie so schlimm, wie man es sich vorstellt."
"I've got to go to the dentist tomorrow. I'm frightened."
"Just keep a stiff upper lip. It's never as bad as one imagines."

Origin: **The picture is of an animal such as a dog or a horse whose ears become erect when it is alert to possible danger.**

bei der Stange bleiben (coll.)

to stick at it (coll.)

Die Arbeit an der Dissertation war schwer und manchmal langweilig, aber Johannes ist bei der Stange geblieben und hat sie zu Ende gebracht.
The work on the dissertation was difficult and sometimes boring but Johannes stuck at it and finished it.

Origin: **A term associated with the horse and carriage. If a carriage was pulled by a team of two horses, they were both harnessed to a shaft (Stange) to ensure that they pulled evenly. If one should break loose from this shaft, the journey would become uncomfortable.**

sich nicht unterkriegen lassen (coll.)

not let something get one down (coll.)

Wegen der abgesagten Urlaubsreise ins Ausland lasse ich mich nicht unterkriegen. Ich erfreue mich genausoviel an den Erholungsmöglichkeiten bei uns im Land.
I won't let the cancelled holiday abroad get me down. I'm just as happy to relax here.

Origin: **From wrestling. The contenders endeavour to bring each other down (unterkriegen).**

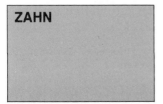

die Zähne zusammenbeißen

to grit one's teeth

Ich ärgerte mich über die Beleidigung, aber ich biß die Zähne zusammen und sagte nichts.
I was annoyed at the insult but I gritted my teeth and said nothing.

16. DIFFICULTIES, UNPLEASANT SITUATIONS

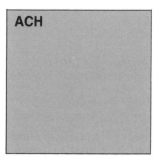

ACH

mit Ach und Krach

with the greatest difficulty, by the skin of one's teeth

Der Lehrling hat die Prüfung sehr schwer gefunden. Er hat sie nur mit Ach und Krach bestanden.
The apprentice found the exam very hard. He only passed it by the skin of his teeth.

Origin: **From the expression 'mit Ächzen und Krächzen' meaning literally 'with groaning and croaking', or, in idiomatic English 'with moans and groans'.**

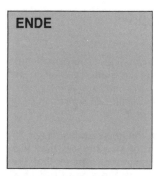

ENDE

Das dicke Ende kommt noch. (coll.)

The worst is yet to come.

Die Reise war schrecklich, und er hat Kopfweh. Aber das dicke Ende kommt noch — alle Hotels im Ort sind völlig ausgebucht!
The journey was awful and he has a headache. But the worst is yet to come — all the hotels in the place are fully booked!

Origin: **From military warfare. At one time when soldiers got to close quarters with the enemy they would turn their rifles round and strike with the butt (das dicke Ende).**

HAKEN

Die Sache hat einen Haken. (coll.)

There's a snag. (coll.)

Ich möchte gerne nach Heidelberg mitfahren. Aber die Sache hat einen Haken — ich habe kein Geld.
I would love to come to Heidelberg with you but there's a snag — I've no money.

Origin: **The reference is to the fisherman's hook concealed in the bait.**

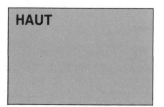

HAUT

nicht in jemandes Haut stecken wollen (coll.)

not to want to be in someone's shoes

Er hat seine Koffer und seinen Reisepaß verloren. Ich möchte nicht in seiner Haut stecken.
He has lost his cases and his passport. I wouldn't like to be in his shoes.

HONIGLECKEN

Das is kein Honiglecken. (coll.)
It's no picnic. (coll.)

Vier Kinder zu erziehen ist kein Honiglecken. Sie nehmen einen ständig in Anspruch.
Bringing up four children is no picnic. They constantly make demands on you.

KLEMME
PATSCHE
TINTE

in der Klemme sitzen (coll.)
in der Patsche sitzen (coll.)
in der Tinte sitzen (coll.)
to be in a fix (coll.)/*jam* (coll.)

Er hat keine Arbeit und kein Geld mehr. Er sitzt ganz schön in der Klemme/Patsche/Tinte.
He has no job and no more money. He's in a real fix.

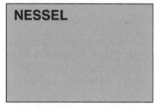

NESSEL

sich in die Nesseln setzen (coll.)
to put oneself in a spot (coll.), *to get into hot water* (coll.)

Er hat gelogen, und der Chef weiß es. Er hat sich schön in die Nesseln gesetzt.
He has lied and the boss knows it. He's really got into hot water.

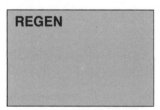

REGEN

vom Regen in die Traufe kommen
to jump out of the frying-pan into the fire

Als er wieder heiratete, kam er vom Regen in die Traufe. Die zweite Ehe war noch unglücklicher als die erste.
When he remarried he jumped out of the frying-pan into the fire. His second marriage was even more unhappy than the first.

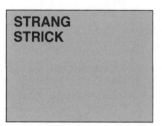

STRANG
STRICK

wenn alle Stränge reißen (coll.)
wenn alle Stricke reißen (coll.)
in the last resort, if the worst comes to the worst

Ich möchte hier arbeiten, aber wenn alle Stricke reißen, werde ich woahders Arbeit suchen.
I would like to work here, but if the worst comes to the worst, I shall look for a job somewhere else.

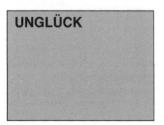

UNGLÜCK

Ein Unglück kommt selten allein. (prov.)
It never rains but it pours. (prov.)

Im Urlaub war das Wetter scheußlich, und auf dem Heimweg hatten sie eine Panne. Ein Unglück kommt selten allein!
On holiday the weather was dreadful, and on the way home they broke down. It never rains but it pours!

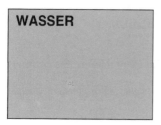

WASSER

Ihm steht das Wasser bis zum Hals.

He's up to his neck in it. (coll.)

Er steckt in Schulden, seine Frau hat ihn verlassen, und er ist Alkoholiker. Ihm steht das Wasser wirklich bis zum Hals.
He's in debt, his wife has left him and he's an alcoholic. He's really up to his neck in it.

17. DISCORD BETWEEN PEOPLE

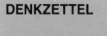

DENKZETTEL

jemandem einen Denkzettel verpassen (coll.)

to teach someone a lesson (coll.)

Wenn der Kerl wieder einmal garstig zu dir ist, werde ich ihm einen Denkzettel verpassen.
If that fellow is nasty to you again I'll teach him a lesson.

Origin: **At one time pupils in Lateinschulen (grammar schools) carried report cards with them on which their misdeeds were recorded. When the card was full the pupils were punished, the memory of which would be unpleasant, hence 'Denkzettel'.**

DORN

jemandem ein Dorn im Auge sein

to be a thorn in someone's side

Die randalierenden Fans waren dem berühmten Fußballverein ein Dorn im Auge. Sie setzten seinen guten Ruf aufs Spiel.
The rioting fans were a thorn in the side of the famous football club. They were putting its good reputation at risk.

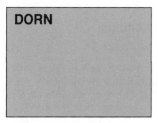

DUNKEL

jemanden im dunkeln lassen

to leave someone in the dark

Ich habe keine Ahnung, was der Johann vorhat. Er läßt mich über seine Pläne völlig im dunkeln.
I have no idea what Johann intends to do. He leaves me completely in the dark about his plans.

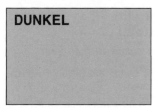

EISEN

jemanden zum alten Eisen werfen

to throw someone on the scrapheap (coll.)

Obgleich er das Pensionsalter schon erreicht hat, will ihn die Firma nicht zum alten Eisen werfen. Durch sein Wissen und seine Erfahrung ist er für sie unentbehrlich.
Although he has reached retirement age the company won't throw him on the scrapheap. Because of his knowledge and experience he is indispensable to them.

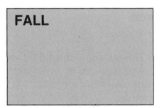

FALL

jemanden zu Fall bringen
to bring someone down

Die hohe Arbeitslosigkeit brachte die Regierung bei den Wahlen zu Fall.
The high rate of unemployment brought the government down at the election.

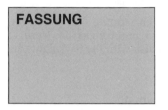

FASSUNG

jemanden aus der Fassung bringen
to put someone off, to throw someone (coll.)

Die unerwartete Frage brachte den Lehrer ganz aus der Fassung. Er wußte nicht, was er darauf antworten sollte.
The unexpected question completely threw the teacher. He did not know what answer he should give.

HAAR

sich (dat.) in den Haaren liegen
to be at loggerheads

Zwei meiner Arbeitskollegen liegen sich ständig in den Haaren. Ich habe mein Möglichstes getan, ein besseres Verständnis zwischen ihnen zu schaffen, aber leider umsonst.
Two of my colleagues at work are constantly at loggerheads. I have done all I could to help them get on with each other, but unfortunately without success.

HANDWERK

jemandem das Handwerk legen
to put a stop to someone's game

Der Buchhalter hat die Firma lange um Geld betrogen, aber endlich konnte man ihm das Handwerk legen.
For a long time the accountant cheated the company of money but finally a stop was put to his game.

Origin: **A medieval guild would bar members from practising their craft if they were found guilty of contravening the guild's regulations. This act of exclusion was called 'das Handwerk legen'.**

KNÜPPEL

jemandem einen Knüppel zwischen die Beine werfen
to put a spoke in someone's wheel

Man hätte mich befördert, aber mein neidischer Kollege hat mir einen Knüppel zwischen die Beine geworfen, indem er mich beim Vorstand schlechtgemacht hat.
I would have got promotion but an envious colleague of mine put a spoke in my wheel by giving me a black name with the management.

jemanden aufs Korn nehmen

to aim at someone

Nach Spielende kritisierte der Trainer die schlechte Leistung unseres Teams, aber alle wußten, daß er besonders mich wegen meiner zwei Eigentore aufs Korn nahm.
At the end of the game the manager criticised the poor performance of our team but everyone knew that his remarks were aimed at me in particular because of my two own goals.

Origin: **From shooting. To get an accurate shot at a target, it has to be in line with the bead, or foresight (das Korn) at the end of the rifle barrel and also with the backsight (die Kimme).**

jemandem den Laufpaß geben

to give someone his marching orders (coll.), *to pack someone in* (coll.)

Ich war völlig überrascht, daß sie Jakobus den Laufpaß gegeben hat. Sie war bis über beide Ohren in ihn verliebt.
I was completely surprised that she gave Jakobus his marching orders. She was madly in love with him.

Origin: **In the 18th century, soldiers leaving the army were given a 'Laufpaß' or 'Laufzettel', a document of recommendation in their search for employment.**

jemanden links liegenlassen
jemanden schneiden

to send someone to Coventry (coll., Br.), *to cut someone dead, to ignore someone*

Weil sich Hannes am Streik nicht beteiligte, ließen ihn seine Arbeitskollegen links liegen/schnitten ihn seine Arbeitskollegen.
Because Hannes did not take part in the strike his workmates cut him dead.

Origin: **a) Links: From an old superstition that the left-hand side is unlucky. b) Schneiden: A literal translation of the English 'to cut a person'.**

jemandem mit gleicher Münze heimzahlen

to pay someone back in his own coin, to give someone tit for tat (coll.)

Mein junger Enkel hat die Luft aus dem Reifen seines Freundes gelassen. Dieser aber hat ihm mit gleicher Münze heimgezahlt und sein Fahrrad versteckt.
My young grandson let the air out of his friend's tyre. The friend paid him back in his own coin, though, and hid my grandson's bike.

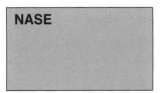

die Nase über jemanden rümpfen

to look down one's nose at someone

Sie rümpft die Nase über Leute, die nicht zu ihrer Gesell-
schaftsklasse gehören.
She looks down her nose at people who are not of her social class.

einen Pik auf jemanden haben (coll.)

*to have a grudge against someone, to have it in for
someone* (coll.)

Seit sie ihm das Geld nicht leihen wollte, hat er einen Pik
auf sie.
*Since she wouldn't lend him the money he's got a grudge against
her.*

Origin: **From the French 'une pique' originally meaning
only 'pike' but which later also adopted the figurative
usage 'a cutting remark'.**

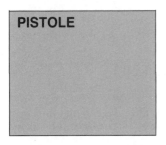

jemandem die Pistole auf die Brust setzen
jemandem die Pistole an die Schläfe setzen

to hold a pistol to someone's head

Weil Kurt sein Taschengeld immer verschwendete, setzten
ihm seine Eltern die Pistole auf die Brust und drohten, ihm
keines mehr zu geben.
*Because Kurt kept wasting his pocket money, his parents held a
pistol to his head and threatened to give him no more.*

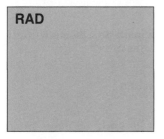

das fünfte Rad am Wagen sein

to be the odd one out, to be a spare part (coll.), *to feel out
of place, to be a fifth wheel* (coll., Am.)

Als die Gesellschaft über Finanzwesen zu sprechen begann, fühlte ich mich wie das fünfte Rad am Wagen. Ich
kenne mich auf diesem Gebiet nicht aus.
*When the group began to talk about finance I felt out of place. I
don't know anything about this subject.*

mit jemandem Schindluder treiben

to take advantage of someone, to misuse someone

Ich will mit dir nicht Schindluder treiben. Wenn du für
mich das Auto reparierst, bekommst du dafür natürlich
bezahlt.
*I don't want to take advantage of you. If you repair the car for me
you will of course be paid for it.*

Origin: **'Das Schindluder' was a dead animal. It was taken
to the knacker's yard to be skinned.**

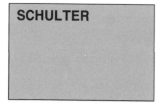

jemandem die kalte Schulter zeigen

to give someone the cold shoulder

Seitdem ich mit ihr Krach gehabt habe, zeigt sie mir die kalte Schulter.
Since I had an argument with her she has given me the cold shoulder.

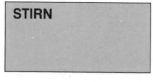

die Stirn haben

to have the nerve, to have the cheek (Br.)

Er hat die Stirn, täglich zu spät zur Arbeit zu kommen.
He has the nerve to arrive late at work every day.

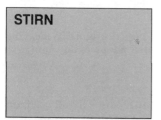

jemandem die Stirn bieten

to defy someone, to stand up to someone

Als der Vorsitzende der Gewerkschaft die Arbeiter zum Streik aufrief, boten sie ihm die Stirn und gingen weiter zur Arbeit.
When the union leader called the workers out on strike, they defied him and carried on working.

über die Stränge schlagen (coll.)

to kick over the traces

Seine Kinder schlagen ständig über die Stränge und horchen nie auf seine Anweisungen. Das macht ihn höchst verlegen, wenn Besuch kommt.
His children constantly kick over the traces and never listen to his instructions. That embarrasses him greatly when visitors come.

Origin: **The reference was originally to a horse wilfully kicking over the traces of its harness.**

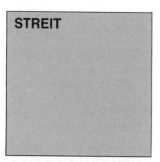

einen Streit vom Zaun brechen

to pick a quarrel

Er ist ein launenhafter Mensch. Er bricht oft ohne Grund einen Streit vom Zaun.
He is a temperamental person. He often picks a quarrel for no reason.

Origin: **From the time when vagabonds would break off a slat from a fence to use it as a threatening weapon when out to rob someone.**

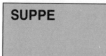

jemandem die Suppe versalzen (coll.)

to spoil things for someone, to put a spoke in someone's wheel

Jetzt Schluß mit der Party! Ich will euch die Suppe nicht versalzen, aber es ist schon spät.
Finish your party now! I don't want to spoil your fun but it's already late.

ÜBRIG

für jemanden nichts übrig haben

to have no time for someone

Für ihn habe ich nichts übrig. Er ist immer so rücksichtslos.
I have no time for him. He is always so inconsiderate.

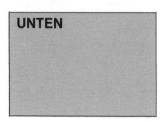

UNTEN

bei jemandem unten durch sein (coll.)

to be out of favour with someone

Weil er ihren Geburtstag vergessen hat, ist er bei ihr unten durch.
Because he forgot her birthday he's out of favour with her.

Origin: **See note on 'Korb' page 52.**

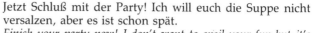

18. DISLIKE

FALL

Das ist nicht mein Fall. (coll.)

That's not my cup of tea. (coll.)

Drachenfliegen ist nicht sein Fall. Er hat eine furchtbare Höhenangst.
Hang-gliding is not his cup of tea. He has a terrible fear of heights.

GESICHT

ein langes Gesicht machen

one's face drops/falls

Als er das Fußballergebnis hörte, machte er ein langes Gesicht.
When he heard the football result, his face dropped.

MARK

jemandem durch Mark und Bein gehen (coll.)

to go right through one (coll.)

Schrei nicht so! Es geht mir durch Mark und Bein.
Don't shout like that! It goes right through me.

PFERD

Keine zehn Pferde bringen mich dahin. (coll.)

Wild horses wouldn't drag me there. (coll.)

Einen Urlaub am Südpol machen! Du bist wohl verrückt. Keine zehn Pferde bringen mich dahin.
A holiday at the South Pole! You must be crazy. Wild horses wouldn't drag me there.

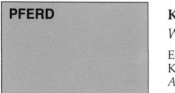

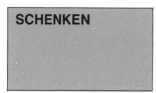

SCHENKEN

sich (dat.) etwas schenken
to give something a miss

Für den Film interessiere ich mich nicht. Den schenke ich mir.
I'm not interested in that film. I'll give it a miss.

19. DISTANCE

FUCHS

wo sich die Füchse gute Nacht sagen
in the back of beyond (coll.), in the middle of nowhere

Wir machen gern Urlaub, wo sich die Füchse gute Nacht sagen. Wir mögen Ruhe und Frieden.
We like to holiday in the middle of nowhere. We like peace and quiet.

HAAR

um ein Haar
by a hair's breadth, by a whisker

Um ein Haar hätte der Ball das Fenster eingeschlagen.
The ball missed smashing the window by a hair's breadth.

HAND

Man sieht die Hand vor den Augen nicht.
You can't see your hand in front of your face.

Bei so dichtem Nebel sieht man die Hand vor den Augen nicht.
In such thick fog you can't see your hand in front of your face.

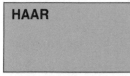

KATZENSPRUNG

ein Katzensprung (coll.)
a stone's throw (coll.)

Von Köln aus können wir schon einen Abstecher nach Bonn machen. Es ist ja nur ein Katzensprung.
From Cologne we can easily pay a visit to Bonn. It's only a stone's throw.

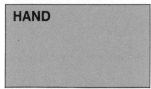

SCHRITT

auf Schritt und Tritt
wherever one goes

Mein Hund folgt mir auf Schritt und Tritt.
My dog follows me wherever I go.

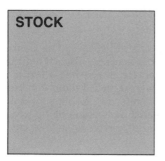

STOCK

über Stock und Stein
up hill and down dale

Die Landschaft war so herrlich, daß wir einfach über Stock und Stein wanderten, ohne uns um ein gewisses Ziel zu kümmern.
The scenery was so magnificent that we simply hiked up hill and down dale without bothering about a definite destination.

Origin: **It was formerly the practice to fill in sodden areas in a roadway with sticks and stones.**

20. ENJOYMENT, HAPPINESS, PLEASURE

ELEMENT

in seinem Element sein
to be in one's element

Wenn Franz über Fußball spricht, ist er ganz in seinem Element.
When Franz talks about football he is completely in his element.

FAHRT
SCHWUNG
TOUREN

in Fahrt kommen (coll.)
in Schwung kommen
auf Touren kommen (coll.)

to get going (coll.), *to get into full swing, to get into one's stride*

Frag Ulrichs Vater nicht nach seinen Jugendstreichen. Wenn er erst richtig in Fahrt/in Schwung/auf Touren kommt, will er nie aufhören, davon zu erzählen.
Don't ask Ulrich's father about his youthful escapades. If he really gets going, he'll never stop talking about them.

Origin: **Touren: 'die Tour' means the revolution of an engine ('rev.'). 'Auf Touren' literally means 'at full revs'.**

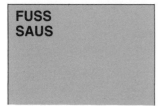

FUSS
SAUS

auf großem Fuß leben
in Saus und Braus leben

to live it up (coll.)

Er lebt im Moment auf großem Fuß/in Saus und Braus. Da seine Firma kurz vor dem Bankrott steht, hört das sicher bald auf.

At the moment he's living it up. As his company is on the verge of bankruptcy that's sure to stop soon.

Origin: **a) Fuß: From the French Middle Ages. The Count of Anjou had long, pointed shoes made for himself to hide the deformity of one of his feet. He established a fashion with this style among people who regarded themselves as noble. b) Saus: Onomatopoeic, referring to the sound of the waves, or of the wind. The picture is of life being lived in a whirl (imagery of the wind), or of 'splashing out' (imagery of the waves).**

HÄUSCHEN

vor Freude aus dem Häuschen sein (coll.)

to be beside oneself with joy

Als die Mannschaft im Pokalendspiel das Siegestor schoß, waren ihre Anhänger vor Freude aus dem Häuschen.
When the team scored the winning goal in the cup final their supporters were beside themselves with joy.

Origin: **The reference is to a state of ecstasy spoken of by mystics in which the soul leaves the body (Häuschen).**

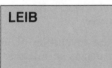

HERAUSGEHEN

aus sich herausgehen

to let one's hair down

Wenn Helene auf Urlaub ist, geht sie immer aus sich heraus. Ohne den Streß in der Arbeit fühlt sie sich entspannt und fröhlich.
When Helene is on holiday she always lets her hair down. Without the stress of her work she feels relaxed and happy.

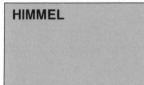

HIMMEL

wie im siebten Himmel sein (coll.)

to be in the seventh heaven (coll.), to be on cloud nine (coll.), to be over the moon (coll.)

Seit ihr Stefan seine Liebe gestand, ist Ruth wie im siebten Himmel.
Since Stefan said he loved her Ruth has been over the moon.

LEIB

mit Leib und Seele

with heart and soul

Mit Leib und Seele bastelte er an seinem Modellflugzeug.
He put his heart and soul into making his model aeroplane.

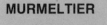

MURMELTIER

wie ein Murmeltier schlafen

to sleep like a log (coll.)

Nach einem langen Spaziergang am Abend schlafe ich immer wie ein Murmeltier.
After a long walk in the evening I always sleep like a log.

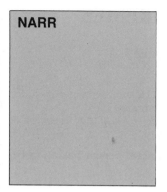

NARR

an jemandem einen Narren gefressen haben (coll.)

to have a crush on someone (coll.), to be infatuated with someone

Viele Mädchen haben an jenem feschen jungen Schlagersänger einen Narren gefressen.
A lot of girls have a crush on that good-looking young pop singer.

Origin: **The picture is of being able to eat someone because he/she is loved so much. A person taken up with someone to such an extent becomes, in this picture, irrational or foolish. The idea, then, is of swallowing a foolish spirit.**

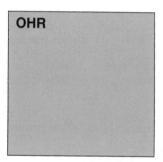

OHR

bis über beide Ohren verliebt sein

to be head over heels in love

Mit Lotte kann man nichts anfangen. Sie ist bis über beide Ohren verliebt und will nichts tun, als sitzen und von ihrem neuen Freund träumen.
We can't do a thing with Lotte. She's head over heels in love and doesn't want to do anything but sit and dream about her new boyfriend.

Origin: **The picture is of someone going under or sinking.**

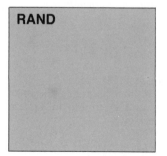

RAND

außer Rand und Band geraten

to be no holding someone (coll.), to go wild (coll.)

Bei seinem Sieg im Titelkampf gerieten die Anhänger des jungen Boxers außer Rand und Band.
At his victory in the title fight the fans of the young boxer went wild.

Origin: **From cooperage. If a barrel has no rim binding (Randeinfassung) at its top and bottom, and no hoop (Band) round its centre, it will fall apart.**

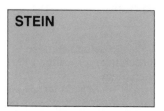

STEIN

Mir fällt ein Stein vom Herzen.

It's a load off my mind.

Als der Lehrer mir sagte, daß ich nicht sitzenbleiben müßte, fiel mir ein Stein vom Herzen.
When the teacher told me that I did not have to repeat the year it was a load off my mind.

21. EXAGGERATION, EXTREMES

HAAR

an den Haaren herbeigezogen

far-fetched

Ich finde dieses Beispiel an den Haaren herbeigezogen. Es dient deiner Argumentation überhaupt nicht.
I find this example far-fetched. It doesn't help your argument at all.

Origin: **The picture is of a reluctant person having to be dragged by the hair.**

STECKNADEL

eine Stecknadel in einem Heuhaufen suchen

to look for a needle in a haystack

Du willst in England nach einem gewissen John Smith suchen? Da suchst du eine Stecknadel in einem Heuhaufen. Tausende von Männern laufen mit diesem Namen herum.
You want to look for a certain John Smith in England? Then you're looking for a needle in a haystack. There are thousands of men with that name.

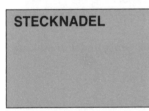

STECKNADEL

so still sein, daß man eine Stecknadel fallen hören könnte

to be so still that you could hear a pin drop

In diesem Wald ist es so still, daß man eine Stecknadel fallen hören könnte.
It's so still in this wood that you could hear a pin drop.

STURM

ein Sturm im Wasserglas

a storm in a teacup

„Hat er mit seiner Frau Krach gehabt?"
„Es war eigentlich nur ein Sturm im Wasserglas. Sie hatte den Hausschlüssel vergessen, und er mußte in seinem neuen Anzug durch ein Fenster klettern."
"Did he have a row with his wife?"
"It was actually only a storm in a teacup. She had forgotten the front door key and he had to climb through a window in his new suit."

TROPFEN

ein Tropfen auf den heißen Stein

a drop in the ocean

Er braucht mehrere tausend Mark, um seine Schulden zu tilgen. Was er gestern beim Pferderennen gewonnen hat, ist nur ein Tropfen auf den heißen Stein.
He needs several thousand marks to clear his debts. What he won on the horses yesterday is only a drop in the ocean.

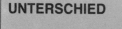

UNTERSCHIED

ein Unterschied wie Tag und Nacht
as different as chalk and cheese (Br.), *as different as day and night* (Am.)

Privat verstehen wir uns ganz gut, aber beruflich sind unsere Ansichten so unterschiedlich wie Tag und Nacht.
Socially we get on quite well but professionally our views are as different as chalk and cheese (or, as day and night).

22. FAILURE

BINSE

in die Binsen gehen (coll.)
to go up in smoke (coll.), *to go for a burton* (coll., Br.)

Seine Pläne, für die Nationalmannschaft spielen zu können, sind durch die erfolglose Operation am Knie in die Binsen gegangen.
His plans for playing in the national team went up in smoke because of the unsuccessful operation on his knee.

Origin: **A hunting term. A wild duck took refuge from the hunter or his dog by hiding in the rushes (Binsen) of a pond or lake.**

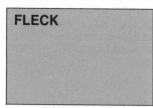

FLECK

nicht vom Fleck kommen
to make no headway

Seine Kinder lassen ihn nicht in Ruhe. Er kommt mit seiner Arbeit nicht vom Fleck.
His children won't leave him in peace. He's making no headway with his work.

GLEIS
PUNKT
SACKGASSE

aufs tote Gleis kommen
auf den toten Punkt kommen
in eine Sackgasse geraten
to come to a dead end

Der Autor ist mit seinem Buch aufs tote Gleis gekommen/auf den toten Punkt gekommen/in eine Sackgasse geraten. Er ist völlig ideenlos.
The author has come to a dead end with his book. He's run right out of ideas.

Origin: a) **Gleis: 'Ein totes Gleis' is a railway siding.**
b) **Punkt: A point at which a steam-engine has insufficient momentum to continue rotating.**

HAUFEN

über den Haufen werfen

to knock on the head (coll.), *to upset* (*someone's plans*)

Unsere Pläne, in Athen Urlaub zu machen, sind durch meine Krankheit über den Haufen geworfen worden.
Our plans for a holiday in Athens have been upset by my illness.

Origin: **The word 'der Haufen' meaning 'heap' suggests things lying on top of each other in disarray. Applied to the field of battle it suggests the disorder and confusion into which the enemy is thrown when close to defeat.**

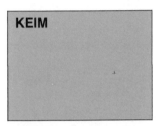

KEIM

etwas im Keim ersticken

to nip something in the bud

Das böswillige Gerücht, daß er seine Katze grausam behandelte, konnte ich im Keim ersticken. Ich weiß, daß er keine hat!
I was able to nip in the bud the malicious rumour that he was cruel to his cat. I know he hasn't got one!

KORB

jemandem einen Korb geben

to turn someone down

Er ist fesch, reich und intelligent, aber trotzdem hat sie ihm einen Korb gegeben. Sie will noch nicht heiraten.
He is good looking, rich and intelligent but she still turned him down. She doesn't want to get married yet.

Origin: **In the Minnesinger period (12th and 13th centuries) a maiden would lower a basket with a weak bottom to an unwanted suitor. On being hauled up to the maiden's window, he would fall through the basket. This, too, is the origin of the idiom 'bei jemandem unten durch sein' (q.v.) and the verb 'durchfallen' meaning 'to fail'.**

KURZ

den kürzeren ziehen

to draw the short straw, to get the worst of something, to come off worst

Er streitet nicht gern mit seiner Schwester. Er zieht immer den kürzeren.
He doesn't like arguing with his sister. He always comes off worst.

Origin: **The drawing of straws was once a method of making decisions. The shorter straw represented an adverse decision.**

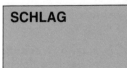

SCHLAG

ein Schlag ins Wasser

a flop

Die neueste Schallplatte von meinem Lieblingssänger war ein Schlag ins Wasser. Sie kam nicht in die Hitparade.

The latest record by my favourite singer was a flop. It didn't make the charts.

Origin: **Striking water has no lasting effect. The ripples subside and the water becomes smooth again.**

STELLE

auf der Stelle treten

to make no headway, to tread water

Im Beruf tritt er seit Jahren auf der Stelle. Das kommt davon, daß er einfach über zu wenig Initiative verfügt.
He has made no headway in his career for years. That's because he has simply too little initiative.

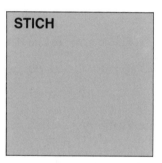

STICH

jemanden im Stich lassen

to let someone down, to leave someone in the lurch

Er braucht dringend deine Hilfe. Laß ihn doch nicht im Stich!
He urgently needs your help. Don't let him down!

Origin: **Several possibilities, but the most likely would appear to be the abandonment of a comrade-in-arms on the field of battle with the result that he would be stabbed by the enemy.**

STRICH

jemandem einen Strich durch die Rechnung machen

to upset someone's plans

Ich wollte heute nach Paris fliegen, aber der Fluglotsen-Streik hat mir einen Strich durch die Rechnung gemacht.
I wanted to fly to Paris today but the air-traffic controllers' strike upset my plans.

Origin: **Here 'Rechnung' does not mean 'bill' but 'calculation' or 'sum'. The reference is to a pupil's incorrect solution of an arithmetic problem being crossed out by the teacher.**

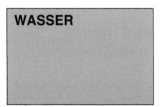

WASSER

ins Wasser fallen (coll.)

to fall through

Das geplante Fußballspiel gegen die Nachbarstadt fiel ins Wasser, weil viele unserer Spieler Grippe hatten.
The planned football match against our neighbouring town fell through because many of our players had 'flu.

23. FEAR

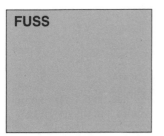

FUSS

kalte Füße bekommen (coll.)

to get cold feet (coll.)

Ich hatte vor, gestern den Direktor meiner Bank um ein weiteres Überziehen meines Kontos zu bitten, aber im letzten Moment bekam ich kalte Füße und tat es nicht.
I had intended to ask my bank manager yesterday for a further overdraft on my account but at the last minute I got cold feet and didn't do it.

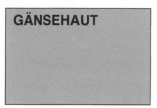

GÄNSEHAUT

eine Gänsehaut bekommen

to get goose-pimples

Als er an seine bevorstehende Prüfung dachte, bekam der Student eine Gänsehaut.
When he thought of his approaching exam the student got goose-pimples.

HAAR

Jemandem stehen die Haare zu Berge.

Someone's hair stands on end.

Es war spät am Abend, und Maria war allein im Haus. Als sie plötzlich eine dunkle Gestalt am Fenster sah, standen ihr die Haare zu Berge.
It was late in the evening and Maria was alone in the house. When she suddenly saw a dark shape at the window her hair stood on end.

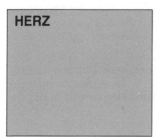

HERZ

Jemandem fällt/rutscht das Herz in die Hose. (coll.)

to have one's heart in one's mouth, one's heart sinks into one's boots (coll.)

Als ich den Löwen auf mich zukommen sah, fiel/rutschte mir das Herz in die Hose.
When I saw the lion coming towards me, my heart sank into my boots.

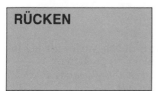

RÜCKEN

Es läuft einem kalt über den Rücken.

Something sends a shiver down one's spine.

In diesem gruseligen Wald läuft es mir kalt über den Rücken.
This eerie forest sends a shiver down my spine.

24. HARMONY BETWEEN PEOPLE

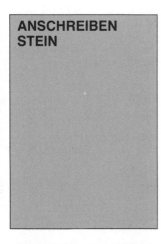

**ANSCHREIBEN
STEIN**

**bei jemandem gut angeschrieben sein (coll.)
bei jemandem einen Stein im Brett haben**

to be in someone's good books, to be well in with someone (coll.)

Norbert ist bei meinem Vater gut angeschrieben/hat bei meinem Vater einen Stein im Brett. Sie sind beide begeisterte Angler.
Norbert is well in with my father. They're both keen fishermen.

Origin: a) **Angeschrieben: If one had no debt chalked up on the landlord's slate, one was said to be 'gut angeschrieben' and therefore in favour with the landlord.
b) Stein: In games such as draughts, one's chances of victory were promising if one could get a piece (Stein) into the back line of the opponent's half of the board (Brett).**

DECKE

mit jemandem unter einer Decke stecken (coll.)

to be in cahoots with someone (coll.), to be hand in glove with someone

Es nützt nichts, dich beim Bürgermeister über das Vorgehen des Gemeinderates zu beklagen. Sie stecken unter einer Decke.
There's no point complaining to the mayor about the action of the councillor. They're hand in glove with each other.

Origin: **A ceremony in which two men became blood brothers. They would enter a 'tent', the cover or ceiling (Decke) of which was made of a broad unbroken strip of turf. It was supported by a spear. In it the two men let a few drops of their blood drip onto the soil from which the turf had been cut, and swore loyalty to each other 'bis uns der Rasen deckt', i.e. unto death.**

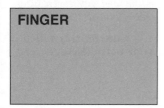

FINGER

jemanden um den kleinen Finger wickeln

to twist someone round one's little finger

Seine Tochter kann ihn um den kleinen Finger wickeln. Alles was sie will, bekommt sie.
His daughter can twist him round her little finger. She gets everything she wants.

FUSS

mit jemandem auf gutem Fuß stehen

to be on good terms with someone

Obgleich andere ihn nicht besonders leiden können, stehe ich mit ihm auf gutem Fuß.
Although others don't really like him, I'm on good terms with him.

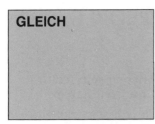

Gleich und gleich gesellt sich gern. (prov.)

Birds of a feather flock together. (prov.)

Es wundert mich nicht, daß der Grobian Gerhard auch unter den randalierenden Fußballfans war. Gleich und gleich gesellt sich gern.
It doesn't surprise me that that lout Gerhard was among the rioting football fans. Birds of a feather flock together.

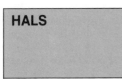

jemandem um den Hals fallen

to fling one's arms around someone's neck

Als sie ihren Vater sah, fiel sie ihm um den Hals.
When she saw her father she flung her arms around his neck.

ein Herz und eine Seele sein

to be bosom pals (coll.)

Karl und Klaus sind ein Herz und eine Seele. Sie unternehmen alles zusammen.
Karl and Klaus are bosom pals. They do everything together.

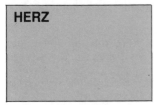

jemanden ins Herz schließen

to take someone to one's heart

Ihr Töchterchen hat ein sehr liebes Wesen. Ich habe sie ins Herz geschlossen.
Your little daughter has a very sweet nature. I've taken her to my heart.

in die gleiche Kerbe hauen

to take the same line

Wenn beide Elternteile nicht in die gleiche Kerbe hauen und gegensätzliche Anweisungen geben, werden ihre Kinder konfus.
If both parents don't take the same line, and give contradictory instructions, their children will become confused.

Origin: **From lumbering. A tree is more quickly felled if the woodcutters chop into the same notch (Kerbe).**

KRIEGSBEIL

das Kriegsbeil begraben

to bury the hatchet

Nach jahrelangem Streit haben die zwei Familien endlich das Kriegsbeil begraben.
After years of squabbling the two families have finally buried the hatchet.

Origin: **From Nordic mythology. Peace between the gods existed as long as Thor's axe remained buried.**

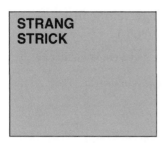

STRANG
STRICK

am gleichen Strang ziehen
am gleichen Strick ziehen
to pull together

„Wenn wir alle im Land am gleichen Strang/Strick ziehen",
sagte der Minister in einem Fernsehinterview, „kommen
wir aus dieser Krise heraus."
*"If we all pull together," said the Minister in a television
interview, "we'll come through this crisis."*

STÜCK

große Stücke auf jemanden halten
to think highly of someone

Die Nachbarn halten große Stücke auf unsere Tochter
Karin, weil sie immer so höflich und freundlich ist. Wir
sind sehr stolz auf sie.
*The neighbours think highly of our daughter Karin because she is
always so polite and friendly. We are very proud of her.*

Origin: **At one time the value of a coin could be gauged by
its size. Large coins (große Stücke) had the greatest pur-
chasing power.**

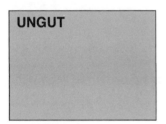

UNGUT

Nichts für ungut.
No harm meant.

„Warum lächelst du mich so an?"
„Nichts für ungut, aber deine Schuhe hast du verkehrt
herum angezogen!"
"Why are you smiling at me like that?"
"No harm meant, but you've got your shoes on the wrong feet!"

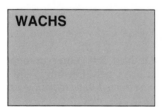

WACHS

Wachs in jemandes Händen sein
to be putty in someone's hands

Er ist ein harter Geschäftsmann, aber zu Hause ist er Wachs
in den Händen seiner vierjährigen Tochter.
*He's a tough businessman but at home he's putty in his four year
old daughter's hands.*

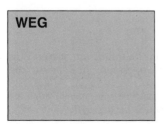

WEG

jemandem auf halbem Weg entgegenkommen
to meet someone halfway

Sie können sich über die Entscheidung nicht völlig einigen,
aber sie sind bereit, sich auf halbem Weg entgegenzukom-
men.
*They cannot fully agree about the decision but they are prepared to
meet each other halfway.*

WELLENLÄNGE

auf der gleichen Wellenlänge sein (coll.)

to be on the same wavelength (coll.)

Josef und Frauke sind auf der gleichen Wellenlänge. Sie verstehen sich fabelhaft.
Josef and Frauke are on the same wavelength. They get on fabulously together.

25. HASTE, SPEED

BEIN

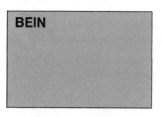

sich auf die Beine machen (coll.)

to make tracks (coll.)

Wir möchten gerne länger bleiben, aber leider müssen wir uns auf die Beine machen.
We would love to stay longer but unfortunately we must make tracks.

BLITZ

wie der Blitz

like lightning

Als Herr Wagner seine Tochter auf der Straße liegen sah, lief er wie der Blitz zu ihr hinüber.
When Herr Wagner saw his daughter lying in the street, he ran across to her like lightning.

EILEN

Eile mit Weile. (prov.)

More haste, less speed. (prov.)

Renn nicht so verrückt herum. Du hast Zeit genug, deinen Koffer zu packen und den Zug zu erreichen. Eile mit Weile.
Don't run around like an idiot. You've enough time to pack your case and to catch the train. More haste, less speed.

HALS

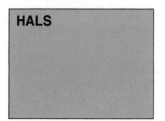

Hals über Kopf (coll.)

in a mad hurry/rush (coll.)

Alfred fuhr Hals über Kopf zum Bahnhof, um seinen Zug noch zu erreichen. Er hatte vergessen, daß heute die Konferenz stattfand.
Alfred drove to the station in a mad hurry in order to catch his train. He had forgotten that today was the day of the conference.

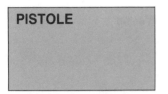

wie aus der Pistole geschossen

like a shot

Wie aus der Pistole geschossen zeigte Edith auf. Sie wußte die Antwort.
Like a shot Edith put her hand up. She knew the answer.

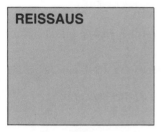

Reißaus nehmen (coll.)

to take to one's heels, to make oneself scarce

Als beim Banküberfall die Alarmanlage zu läuten begann, nahmen die Einbrecher Reißaus.
When the alarm began to sound during the bank raid, the burglars made themselves scarce.

Origin: **From the verb 'ausreißen' meaning 'to run off'.**

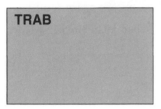

jemanden auf Trab bringen (coll.)

to make someone get a move on (coll.)

Wenn du Heidi nicht auf Trab bringst, versäumen wir die Theateraufführung.
If you don't make Heidi get a move on we'll miss the theatre performance.

26. HEALTH, SICKNESS

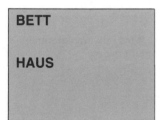

das Bett hüten müssen

to be confined to bed, to have to stay in bed

das Haus hüten müssen

to be confined to the house, to have to stay in the house

Unser Onkel hat eine Grippe und muß das Bett hüten.
Our uncle has 'flu and has to stay in bed.

Was fehlt Ihnen denn?

What's up with you, then? (coll., Br.) *What's wrong with you?*

„Was fehlt Ihnen denn?" fragte mich der Arzt, als er mich im Bett liegen sah.
"What's up with you, then?" the doctor asked me when he saw me lying in bed.

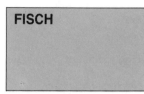

FISCH

gesund wie ein Fisch im Wasser
as fit as a fiddle

Trotz seines hohen Alters ist er gesund wie ein Fisch im Wasser.
In spite of his great age he is as fit as a fiddle.

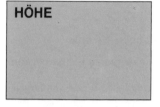

HÖHE

nicht ganz auf der Höhe sein
to be a bit under the weather (coll.), *to be a bit off colour* (coll.)

Ich bin heute nicht ganz auf der Höhe. Ich bleibe lieber im Bett.
I'm a bit off colour today. I think I'd better stay in bed.

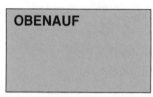

OBENAUF

wieder obenauf sein
to be back to normal, to be back on top again (coll.)

Letzte Woche war ich krank, aber jetzt bin ich wieder obenauf.
Last week I was ill but now I'm back to normal again.

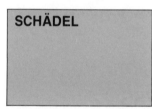

SCHÄDEL

Mir brummt der Schädel.
My head is throbbing.

Die Jugendlichen im Nachbarhaus haben so laut Platten gespielt, daß mir der Schädel brummt.
The young people next door have been playing their records so loudly that my head is throbbing.

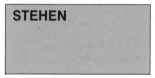

STEHEN

Wie steht es um jemanden?
What is someone's condition? How is someone doing?

Wie steht es um den Patienten? Wird er durchkommen?
How is the patient doing? Will he pull through?

27. HELP, ASSISTANCE

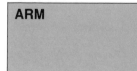

ARM

jemandem unter die Arme greifen
to help someone out

Als er neulich in finanzielle Schwierigkeiten geriet, griff ihm sein Freund unter die Arme.

When he recently got into financial difficulties, his friend helped him out.

Origin: **Support given to someone about to fall, e.g. an injured knight in a tournament.**

BRESCHE

für jemanden in die Bresche springen

to step into the breach

Unsere Babysitterin wurde plötzlich krank, aber glücklicherweise konnte unsere Nachbarin im letzten Moment für sie in die Bresche springen.
Our babysitter suddenly became ill, but fortunately our neighbour could step into the breach at the last minute.

Origin: **A breach was a gap in a military line of defence. Another soldier would have to step into it to replace the one who had fallen.**

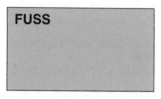

FUSS

jemanden auf freien Fuß setzen

to set someone free

Nach zwei Jahren Haft wurde der Einbrecher auf freien Fuß gesetzt.
After two years imprisonment the burglar was set free.

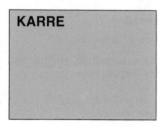

KARRE

die Karre aus dem Dreck ziehen (coll.)

to put things right, to sort things out

Mein Arbeitskollege ist wirklich unzuverlässig. Wenn er etwas verpfuscht, muß immer i c h die Karre aus dem Dreck ziehen.
My workmate is really unreliable. When he bungles something I'm always the one who has to sort things out.

RÜCKEN

jemandem den Rücken stärken

to give someone encouragement

Du mußt ihr den Rücken stärken, bevor sie zu ihrem Vorstellungsgespräch geht.
You've got to give her encouragement before she goes to her interview.

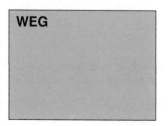

WEG

jemandem den Weg ebnen

to pave the way for someone

Andreas wollte Eleonore um eine Verabredung bitten. Ich habe ihm den Weg geebnet und ihr gesagt, er interessiere sich für sie.
Andreas wanted to ask Eleonore for a date. I paved the way for him and told her that he was interested in her.

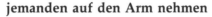

28. HUMOUR, LAUGHTER, RIDICULE, TEASING

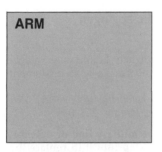

ARM

jemanden auf den Arm nehmen

to pull someone's leg

Peter will nach Wien fliegen? Du nimmst mich wohl auf den Arm — er hat eine furchtbare Höhenangst.
Peter wants to fly to Vienna? You're pulling my leg, aren't you? — He has a terrible fear of heights.

Origin: **When having fun with a small child, one often picks it up in one's arms.**

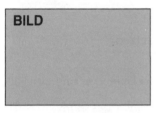

BILD

ein Bild für Götter sein

to be a perfect sight (coll.), *What a sight!* (coll.)

Seht mal! Unser Lehrer trägt zum Spaß eine kupferrote Perücke. Das ist ein Bild für Götter.
Just look! Our teacher is wearing a ginger wig for a joke. What a sight!

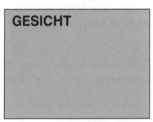

GESICHT

jemandem ein Gesicht schneiden

to make (Am.)/ *pull* (Br.) *a face at someone*

Als Friedl ihre Freundin Astrid sah, schnitt sie ihr ein Gesicht. Sie hatten sich nämlich wegen eines Jungen gestritten.
When Friedl saw her friend Astrid, she pulled (or, made) a face at her. You see, they'd had an argument over a boy.

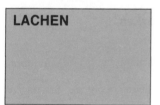

LACHEN

Jemand hat gut lachen. (coll.)

It's all very well for one to laugh.

Du hast gut lachen. Du brauchst diese schwierige Übersetzung nicht zu machen.
It's all very well for you to laugh. You don't have to do this difficult translation.

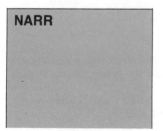

NARR

jemanden zum Narren halten

to make a fool of someone

Der Autohändler hat mich ganz schön zum Narren gehalten. Das Auto, das er mir so leidenschaftlich empfohlen hat, ist ständig in Reparatur!
The car dealer has made a proper fool of me. The car that he so passionately recommended to me is always in for repair!

Origin: **The expression was formerly 'jemanden als Narren (unter)halten' meaning 'to employ someone as a jester'. Jesters were commonly employed in aristocratic households.**

SCHABERNACK
SCHNIPPCHEN
STREICH

mit jemandem Schabernack treiben
jemandem ein Schnippchen schlagen (coll.)
jemandem einen Streich spielen
to play a trick on someone

Jedes Jahr am ersten April treiben meine Kinder mit mir Schabernack/schlagen mir meine Kinder ein Schnippchen/spielen mir meine Kinder einen Streich.
Every year on April the first my children play a trick on me.

Origin: a) **Schabernack: Many centuries ago it was considered outrageous to shave the hair from the nape of the neck (den Nacken schaben). b) Schnippchen: About 1500 a snap of the fingers (Schnippchen) at someone was a way of showing one's superiority over him.**

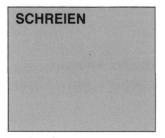

SCHREIEN

Etwas ist zum Schreien. (coll.)
Something is too funny for words. Something is a scream. (coll.)

Gestern zeigte uns unser Vater einige Aufnahmen aus seiner Kindheit. Seine Kleidung war wirklich zum Schreien.
Yesterday our father showed us some photographs from his childhood. His clothes were a scream.

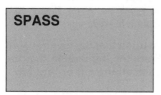

SPASS

keinen Spaß verstehen
not to be able to take a joke

Sein Rad sollten wir lieber nicht verstecken. Er versteht keinen Spaß.
We'd better not hide his bike. He can't take a joke.

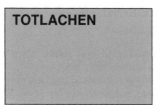

TOTLACHEN

sich totlachen (coll.)
to split one's sides with laughter

Als der Clown in den Eimer Wasser fiel, lachte sich das ganze Publikum tot.
When the clown fell into the bucket of water, the whole audience split its sides with laughter.

29. IDEAS, SUGGESTIONS

EINTRICHTERN

jemandem etwas eintrichtern (coll.)

to drum something into someone (coll.)

Ich habe meinem Sohn eingetrichtert, daß er rücksichtsvoll fahren soll.
I've drummed it into my son that he should drive with consideration.

Origin: **From 'der Trichter' = the funnel.**

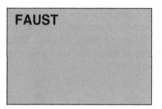

FAUST

auf eigene Faust

off one's own bat (coll.), *on one's own initiative*

Der Dankbrief an unseren Gastgeber war nicht meine Idee. Den schrieben die Kinder auf eigene Faust.
The letter of thanks to our host was not my idea. The children wrote it on their own initiative.

FINGER

LUFT

sich (dat.) etwas aus den Fingern saugen

to make something up, to pull something out of thin air

aus der Luft gegriffen

made up, pure fabrication

Richard will behaupten, die Nordwand des Eigers bestiegen zu haben? Das hat er sich sicher aus den Fingern gesogen./Das ist sicher aus der Luft gegriffen.
Richard claims he has climbed the north face of the Eiger? He's definitely made that up./That's definitely made up.

Origin: **a) Finger: An old superstition that the fingers could impart knowledge. b) Luft: From the impression that the conjuror makes of producing something out of thin air.**

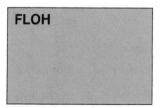

FLOH

jemandem einen Floh ins Ohr setzen

to put ideas into someone's head

Tanzen gehen? Ausgeschlossen! Ingrid soll heute abend Vokabeln lernen. Setz ihr bitte keinen Floh ins Ohr.
Go dancing? Out of the question! Ingrid is supposed to be learning vocabulary this evening. Please don't put ideas into her head.

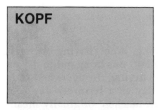

sich (dat.) etwas aus dem Kopf schlagen

to put something out of one's mind

Nach München trampen? Diese Idee kannst du dir gleich aus dem Kopf schlagen. Du bist viel zu jung.
Hitch-hike to Munich? You can put that idea straight out of your mind. You're much too young.

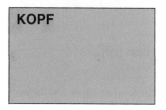

sich (dat.) etwas in den Kopf setzen

to take something into one's head

Er hat es sich in den Kopf gesetzt, seine Stelle zu wechseln. Er will mehr Geld.
He's taken it into his head to change his job. He wants more money.

30. IDLENESS

etwas auf die lange Bank schieben (coll.)

to put something off (coll.)

Wenn du die nötige Reparatur an deinem Auto ständig auf die lange Bank schiebst, wirst du damit bestimmt eine Panne haben.
If you keep putting off the necessary repairs to your car, it will certainly break down.

Origin: **In court, case files that were required immediately were placed next to the lawyer on his bench. Less urgently required files were placed further away on the same bench. Hence the former were referred to as being on the 'kurze Bank', the latter on the 'lange Bank'.**

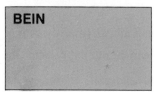

sich (dat.) kein Bein ausreißen (coll.)

not to strain oneself (coll.)

Wenn Günther im Garten arbeitet, reißt er sich kein Bein aus.
When Günther works in the garden he doesn't strain himself.

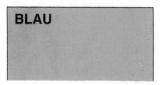

blau machen (coll.)

to skip work (coll.)

Unser Nachbar wollte gestern zu dem großen Pferderennen gehen und hat einfach blau gemacht.

Our neighbour wanted to go to the big horse race yesterday and simply skipped work.

Origin: **A term from wool-dyeing. Wool, having been left to soak in a blue dye on a Sunday, was hung out to dry on a Monday. While the wool was drying, the dyers had little to do, and so regarded Monday as a leisurely day (der blaue Montag). Similarly 'blau machen' originally meant 'to take things easy'.**

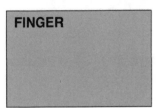

FINGER

keinen Finger krumm machen (coll.)

not to lift a finger (coll.)

Er weiß, wieviel Arbeit wir haben, aber er macht keinen Finger krumm.
He knows how much work we have to do, but he isn't lifting a finger.

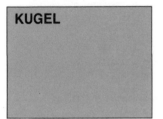

KUGEL

eine ruhige Kugel schieben (coll.)

to have it easy (coll.), *to have a cushy number* (coll., Br.)

Manche behaupten, daß Lehrer in England wegen der langen Ferien eine ruhige Kugel schieben.
Many people maintain that teachers in England have it easy because of the long holidays.

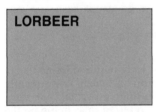

LORBEER

sich auf seinen Lorbeeren ausruhen

to rest on one's laurels

Dieser Fußballklub ruht sich nie auf seinen Lorbeeren aus. Nach jedem Titelgewinn bemüht er sich um den nächsten.
This football club never rests on its laurels. After each title victory it goes after the next one.

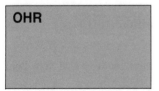

OHR

mit halbem Ohr zuhören

to half listen, to listen with half an ear (mainly Am.)

Ihr werdet wenig verstehen, wenn ihr nur mit halbem Ohr zuhört.
You'll understand little if you only half listen.

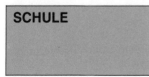

SCHULE

die Schule schwänzen (coll.)

to play truant, to play hooky (Am.)

Jemand, der ständig die Schule schwänzt, lernt nichts.
Someone who constantly plays truant learns nothing.

══ 31. INDEFINITENESS, UNCERTAINTY ══

FADEN

an einem seidenen Faden hängen
to hang by a thread

Sein Leben hängt an einem seidenen Faden. Wenn er nicht bald eine neue Niere bekommt, stirbt er bestimmt.
His life is hanging on a thread. If he doesn't get a new kidney soon, he will certainly die.

Origin: **An ancient Germanic belief that human life was suspended by a thread woven by the goddesses of destiny. The length of a person's life was determined by the thickness of the thread. Hence a** *silk* **thread represented the danger of an imminent death.**

HUPFEN
JACKE

Das ist gehupft wie gesprungen. (coll.)
Das ist Jacke wie Hose. (coll.)
It makes no difference. It's six of one and half a dozen of the other.

„Willst du ins Museum gehen oder in die Kunstgalerie?" „Das ist gehupft wie gesprungen/Jacke wie Hose. Sie wären mir gleich interessant."
"Do you want to go to the museum or the art gallery?"
"It makes no difference. I would find them both equally interesting."

Origin: **Jacke/Hose: The two garments are seen here as being made of the same material.**

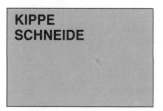
KIPPE
SCHNEIDE

auf der Kippe stehen
auf des Messers Schneide stehen
to be in the balance, to be touch and go

Es steht noch auf der Kippe/auf des Messers Schneide, ob wir unsere Pläne fallenlassen oder nicht.
It's still in the balance whether we cancel our plans or not.

SCHWEBE

in der Schwebe sein
to be in the melting pot

Ob wir an die italienische oder spanische Küste fahren oder gar zu Hause bleiben, ist in der Schwebe. Es kommt darauf an, ob wir zu diesem späten Zeitpunkt noch ein Hotel bekommen.
Whether we go to the Italian or the Spanish coast or even stay at home is in the melting pot. It all depends on whether we can still get a hotel at this late stage.

32. KNOWLEDGE, INFORMATION, COMMUNICATION

BERG

mit etwas hinterm Berg halten

to keep something to oneself

Er ist nicht einer, der mit seiner Meinung hinterm Berg hält. Er sagt einem ins Gesicht, was er denkt.
He is not one to keep his opinion to himself. He'll tell you to your face what he thinks.

Origin: **A most effective way of surprising the enemy in battle was to be concealed behind a hill and to strike at the most opportune moment.**

**HALS
KEHLE**

**etwas in den falschen Hals kriegen
etwas in die falsche Kehle kriegen**

to take something the wrong way

Meine Bemerkung, daß sie eine lustige Frisur hätte, hat sie in den falschen Hals/in die falsche Kehle gekriegt. Ich habe sie als Kompliment, nicht als Beleidigung gemeint.
She took my comment about her having an amusing hairstyle the wrong way. I meant it as a compliment, not as an insult.

Origin: **The picture is of food going down the wrong way, i.e. down the windpipe instead of the gullet.**

LAUFEND

jemanden auf dem laufenden halten

to keep someone informed, to keep someone posted (coll.)

Halt mich über seine Fortschritte auf dem laufenden. Ich bin überzeugt, daß etwas Großes aus ihm wird.
Keep me informed about his progress. I am convinced that he's going to be big one day.

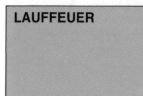

LAUFFEUER

sich wie ein Lauffeuer verbreiten

to spread like wildfire

Die Nachricht, daß unser Nachbar eine Million Mark im Toto gewonnen hatte, verbreitete sich wie ein Lauffeuer.
The news that our neighbour had won a million marks on the pools spread like wildfire.

**LEIER
PLATTE
WALZE**

**immer die alte Leier (coll.)
immer die alte Platte (coll.)
immer die alte Walze (coll.)**

the same old story (coll.)

„Warum hat dein Mann im Berufsleben keine Fortschritte gemacht?"

„Immer die alte Leier/Platte/Walze — er will seine Heimat nicht verlassen, um anderswo Gelegenheiten zu ergreifen."

"Why hasn't your husband made any progress in his career?"

"The same old story — he won't leave his home town to take up opportunities elsewhere."

Origin: **'Die Leier' is a barrel-organ (or hurdy-gurdy). It possesses only a limited repertoire of melodies, and therefore plays the same ones again and again.**

LIED

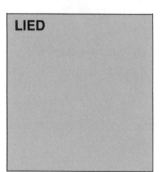

Er weiß ein Lied davon zu singen.

He can tell you a thing or two about it. (coll.)

Mit unartigen Schülern ins Ausland zu fahren, ist wirklich keine Freude. Frag mal den Französischlehrer — er weiß ein Lied davon zu singen.

It's no joy at all going abroad with badly behaved pupils. Ask the French teacher — he can tell you a thing or two about it.

Origin: **Old German folk songs usually had an unhappy ending. Hence idioms containing the word 'Lied' are associated with an unhappy outcome.**

SCHLICH

jemandem auf die Schliche kommen

to get wise to someone

Es war mir völlig schleierhaft, warum Herr Müller immer wieder Geschäftsreisen nach Tübingen machte. Dann bin ich ihm auf die Schliche gekommen — er hatte dort eine Freundin.

I could never understand why Herr Müller kept making business trips to Tübingen. Then I got wise to him — he had a girlfriend there.

Origin: **From hunting. The huntsman gets to know the secret paths (die Schliche) used by animals.**

SCHWARZ

schwarz auf weiß stehen

to be in black and white

Dort steht es schwarz auf weiß — RAUCHEN VERBOTEN!

It's there in black and white — NO SMOKING!

SPATZ

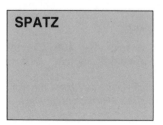

Die Spatzen pfeifen es von den Dächern.

That's common knowledge. It's all over town. (coll.)

Es ist noch nicht offiziell angekündigt worden, daß im Ort ein neues Freizeitzentrum erbaut wird, aber die Spatzen pfeifen es schon von den Dächern.

It hasn't yet been announced officially that a new leisure centre is going to be built in town but it's already common knowledge.

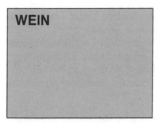

jemandem reinen Wein einschenken

to come clean with someone

Ich möchte dir reinen Wein einschenken: Ich bin kein Großgrundbesitzer, und ich habe keinen Rolls-Royce. Ich wollte dir nur imponieren.
I would like to come clean with you: I'm not a big landowner and I don't have a Rolls Royce. I only wanted to impress you.

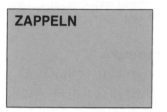

jemanden zappeln lassen (coll.)

to keep someone in suspense, to keep someone on tenterhooks

Laß mich nicht zappeln. Bin ich durchgekommen oder nicht?
Don't keep me in suspense. Did I pass or not?

33. LUCK

es darauf ankommen lassen

to chance it (coll.), to take a chance, to push one's luck (coll.)

Wenn du bei so schlechtem Wetter bergsteigen gehst, passiert dir bestimmt was. Laß es nicht darauf ankommen!
If you go climbing in such bad weather you're bound to have an accident. Don't push your luck!

jemandem die Daumen drücken

to keep one's fingers crossed for someone

Ich drücke dir die Daumen, daß das Prüfungsergebnis gut ausfällt.
I'll keep my fingers crossed that your exam results are good.

Origin: **From the ancient Germanic belief that the thumb symbolised a malicious demon, and that by squeezing the thumb within the four fingers of the hand the demon's power could be restricted.**

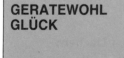

aufs Geratewohl
auf gut Glück

on the off-chance, to take a chance

Wir hatten uns in der Stadt verirrt, aber aufs Geratewohl/auf gut Glück bogen wir in eine Straße ein, die uns dann schließlich ans Ziel führte.
We'd got lost in the town but on the off-chance we turned into (or, we took a chance and turned into) a street which eventually led us to our destination.

Hals- und Beinbruch!

Good luck! Break a leg! (coll., Am.)

Also heute machst du den Führerschein. Hals- und Beinbruch!
So you're taking your driving test today. Good luck!

Origin: **An old superstition held that wicked spirits were irresistibly drawn by well-wishing, as it presented them with an opportunity to cause upset. In an attempt to deceive the spirits, people wished one another the opposite of what was really desired.**

das große Los ziehen

to hit the jackpot (coll.)

Mit seiner Frau Eveline hat der Peter wirklich das große Los gezogen. Sie ist für ihn die perfekte Partnerin.
Peter has really hit the jackpot with his wife Eveline. She is the perfect partner for him.

34. MONEY

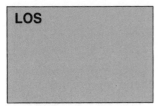

für einen Appel und ein Ei (coll.)
für ein Butterbrot (coll.)

for next to nothing (coll.), *for peanuts* (coll.)

Ich habe dieses schöne Gemälde für einen Appel und ein Ei/für ein Butterbrot gekauft.
I bought this beautiful painting for next to nothing.

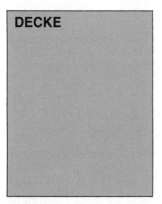

sich nach der Decke strecken

to cut one's coat according to one's cloth, to live within one's means

Wir können uns nicht alle Geräte leisten, die für den Haushalt nützlich wären. Wir müssen uns nach der Decke strecken und nur die allernötigsten kaufen.
We cannot afford all the appliances that would be useful in the home. We'll have to cut our coats according to our cloth and only buy the most necessary.

Origin: **If the bed-cover (die Decke) is too short, one would have to curl up in such a way that one's feet were not exposed.**

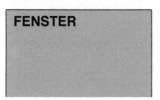

das Geld zum Fenster hinauswerfen

to pour money down the drain

Kauf deiner Nichte das teure Spielzeug nicht. In zwei Wochen wird sein Reiz schon vorbei sein, und dann ist dein Geld zum Fenster hinausgeworfen.

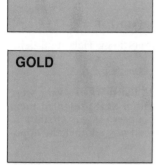

Don't buy your niece that expensive toy. In two weeks its novelty will have worn off and then your money will have been poured down the drain.

GOLD

nicht mit Gold zu bezahlen sein

to be priceless, to be beyond price, to be worth its weight in gold

Was hätte ich ohne dich gemacht? Deine Hilfe und Unterstützung sind nicht mit Gold zu bezahlen.
What would I have done without you? Your help and support are beyond price.

GÜRTEL

den Gürtel enger schnallen

to tighten one's belt

Wegen der Inflation sind die Lebenshaltungskosten gestiegen. Wir müssen jetzt den Gürtel enger schnallen.
Because of inflation the cost of living has risen. We'll have to tighten our belts.

HAND

von der Hand in den Mund leben

to live from hand to mouth

Seit unser Vater arbeitslos ist, müssen wir von der Hand in den Mund leben.
Since our father has been unemployed we've had to live from hand to mouth.

HEU

Geld wie Heu haben (coll.)

to have pots of money (coll.)

Ich kann es mir nicht leisten, zweimal im Jahr ins Ausland zu fahren. Geld wie Heu habe ich nicht.
I can't afford to go abroad twice a year. I haven't got pots of money.

KANTE

etwas auf die hohe Kante legen (coll.)

to save something for a rainy day (coll.)

Ich gebe nie mein ganzes Geld aus, sondern lege immer einen Teil davon auf die hohe Kante.
I never spend all my money but save some of it for a rainy day.

Origin: **When coins are stored, they are packed in rolls of paper and then placed high up on a ledge (Kante).**

KREIDE

bei jemandem tief in der Kreide stehen (coll.)

to be deep in debt to someone

Beim Metzger steht sie schon tief in der Kreide. Sie bekommt jetzt keinen Kredit mehr.

She's already deep in debt to the butcher. She won't get any more credit now.

Origin: **From the practice of a landlord chalking a guest's debts on a slate.**

OHR

bis über beide Ohren in Schulden stecken (coll.)
to be up to one's ears in debt (coll.)

Die neue Waschmaschine können wir uns unmöglich leisten. Wir stecken ja schon bis über beide Ohren in Schulden.
We can't possibly afford the new washing machine. We're already up to our ears in debt.

Origin: **The picture is of someone going under or sinking.**

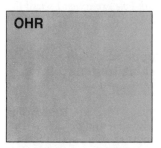

PLEITE

pleite sein (coll.)
to be broke (coll.)

Ich möchte gerne dieses Buch kaufen, aber leider bin ich pleite.
I would love to buy this book, but unfortunately I'm broke.

Origin: **From Hebrew 'peleta' meaning 'flight'. This became 'pleto' in Yiddish with the additional meaning of 'bankruptcy'. The connection between 'flight' and 'bankruptcy' is probably explained from the fact that flight was the surest way for a bankrupt person to evade the demands of his creditors.**

VERHÄLTNIS

über seine Verhältnisse leben
to live beyond one's means

Kein Wunder, daß er nie Geld hat. Er lebt ständig über seine Verhältnisse.
It's no wonder that he never has money. He constantly lives beyond his means.

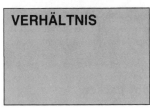

35. OPPORTUNITY, CHANCE

EISEN

Das Eisen schmieden, solange es heiß ist. (prov.)
Strike while the iron is hot. (prov.) Make hay while the sun shines. (prov.)

Kauf dir heute noch das Auto. Ab morgen steigen die Preise. Man soll das Eisen schmieden, solange es heiß ist.
Buy the car today. Tomorrow the prices are going up. One should strike while the iron is hot.

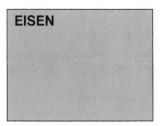

HAND
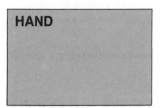

mit beiden Händen zugreifen

to seize the opportunity with both hands

Als man mich einlud, an der Südpolexpedition teilzunehmen, griff ich mit beiden Händen zu.
When I was invited to join the South Pole expedition I seized the opportunity with both hands.

KLAPPE
SCHLAG

zwei Fliegen mit einer Klappe schlagen (coll.)
zwei Fliegen mit einem Schlag treffen (coll.)

to kill two birds with one stone (coll.)

Nächste Woche in London schlage ich zwei Fliegen mit einer Klappe. Ich werde einen alten Freund besuchen und auch zum ersten Mal die Westminster-Abtei besichtigen.
I shall kill two birds with one stone in London next week. I shall visit an old friend and also see Westminster Abbey for the first time.

LUFT
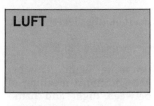

Die Luft ist rein.

The coast is clear.

„Die Luft ist rein", sagte der Bankräuber. „Los, verschwinden wir!"
"The coast is clear," said the bank robber. "Quick, let's go!"

SAGEN
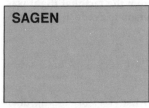

sich (dat.) etwas nicht zweimal sagen lassen

not need to be told twice

Als der Direktor den Schülern sagte, sie dürften frühzeitig nach Hause gehen, ließen sie sich es nicht zweimal sagen.
When the headmaster told the pupils they could go home early, they didn't need to be told twice.

SCHOPF
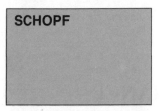

die Gelegenheit beim Schopf packen

to jump at the opportunity

Sein Opa packte die Gelegenheit beim Schopf, zum ersten Mal eine Flugreise machen zu können.
His grandad jumped at the opportunity of being able to travel by air for the first time.

SPATZ

Besser ein Spatz in der Hand als eine Taube auf dem Dach. (prov.)

A bird in the hand is worth two in the bush. (prov.)

Diese Stelle nehme ich an, anstatt auf eine einträglichere zu warten. Besser ein Spatz in der Hand als eine Taube auf dem Dach.
I'll accept this job rather than wait for a better paid one. A bird in the hand is worth two in the bush.

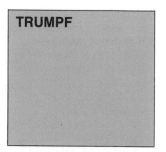

TRUMPF

einen Trumpf ausspielen

to play one's trump card

Zuerst wollte ich das Auto nicht kaufen, aber dann hat der Autohändler einen Trumpf ausgespielt. Er hat gesagt, daß die Werkstätte für alle Reparaturen in den nächsten zwei Jahren verantwortlich sein würde.
At first I didn't want to buy the car but then the car dealer played his trump card. He said that the garage would be responsible for all repairs in the next two years.

WERDEN

Was nicht ist, kann noch werden. (prov.)

Your day will come.

Laß dich nicht davon unterkriegen, daß du für die Nationalmannschaft nicht aufgestellt worden bist. Du bist noch jung. Was nicht ist, kann noch werden.
Don't let it get you down that you haven't been selected for the national team. You're still young. Your day will come.

36. OUTCOME, UPSHOT, RESULT

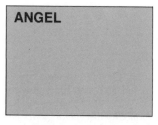

ANGEL

die Welt aus den Angeln heben

to turn the world upside down

Die neue Mikrochip-Technik hebt die Welt aus den Angeln. Maschinen ersetzen weitgehend menschliche Arbeitskräfte.
The new microchip technology is turning the world upside down. Machines are taking the place of human labour on a wide scale.

AUGE

mit einem blauen Auge davonkommen

to get off lightly

Horst hatte seine Hausaufgaben nicht gemacht, und als Strafe hat ihn der Lehrer eine halbe Stunde nachsitzen lassen. Er ist mit einem blauen Auge davongekommen — meistens muß man eine Stunde nachsitzen.
Horst hadn't done his homework and as a punishment the teacher gave him half an hour's detention. He got off lightly — usually detention lasts an hour.

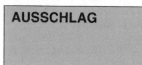

AUSSCHLAG

den Ausschlag geben

to clinch something (coll.), to be the decisive factor, to tip the scales

Am Anfang war er unsicher, ob er mit seinen Freunden ins Theater gehen wollte, aber daß seine Freundin Adele versprach mitzugehen, gab bei ihm den Ausschlag.
To start with he wasn't sure if he wanted to go to the theatre with his friends, but the fact that his girlfriend Adele promised to come with them clinched it for him.

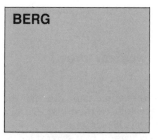

BERG

über den Berg sein

to have broken the back of something (coll.)*, to have turned the corner, to be over the hill*

Ich habe noch eine Menge Arbeit, aber wenn das Schlafzimmer fertig tapeziert ist, werde ich damit über den Berg sein.
I still have a lot of work to do, but when I've finished papering the bedroom I'll have turned the corner.

BILDFLÄCHE

von der Bildfläche verschwinden

to disappear from the scene

Er saß ruhig im Wohnzimmer und las die Zeitung, aber als er durch das Fenster das Auto seiner Schwiegermutter erblickte, verschwand er von der Bildfläche.
He was sitting quietly in the lounge reading the paper but when he caught sight of his mother-in-law's car, he disappeared from the scene.

BLATT

Das Blatt hat sich gewendet.

The tide has turned.

In der ersten Saisonhälfte hat unser Ortsverein viele Spiele verloren, aber seit Weihnachten hat sich das Blatt gewendet, und er gewinnt nun immer.
In the first half of the season our local club lost many games but since Christmas the tide has turned and now they're winning all the time.

Origin: **From card playing. After a bad run, a player suddenly receives a good hand (Blatt), or vice versa.**

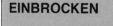

EINBROCKEN

Was man sich (dat.) eingebrockt hat, das muß man auch auslöffeln. (prov.)

You've made your bed, now you must lie on it. (coll.)

Beklag dich nicht, daß hier im Ort nicht viel los ist. Es war d e i n e Entscheidung, dein sehr geselliges Leben in der Stadt aufzugeben und aufs Land zu ziehen. Was man sich eingebrockt hat, das muß man auch auslöffeln.
Don't complain that there isn't much life here. It was your decision to give up your social life in the city and move to the country. You've made your bed, now you must lie on it.

EIS

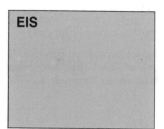

etwas auf Eis legen

to put on ice

Unsere Reisepläne müssen wir auf Eis legen, weil wir eben ein neues Baby bekommen haben.
We'll have to put our travel plans on ice because we've just had a new baby.

Origin: **From cookery. What is put on ice is preserved.**

ENDE

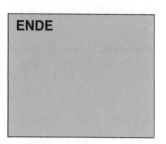

Ende gut, alles gut. (prov.)

All's well that ends well. (prov.)

Rudolf hat seinen Zug verpaßt, aber ganz unerwartet fuhr sein Freund Alex vor und brachte ihn noch rechtzeitig zum Spielbeginn. Ende gut, alles gut.
Rudolf missed his train but quite unexpectedly his friend Alex drove up and got him to the start of the game on time. All's well that ends well.

ENDE

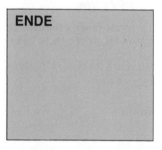

das Ende vom Lied

the outcome, the upshot of this

Beim Abitur fiel Oskar in Chemie durch. Das Ende vom Lied war, daß er sein Hochschulstudium nicht antreten konnte.
In the Abitur examination Oskar failed in chemistry. The upshot of this was that he couldn't begin his university course.

Origin: **German folk songs often had unhappy endings.**

FERTIG

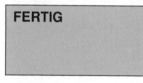

ganz fertig sein (coll.)

to be all in (coll.), *to be shattered* (coll.)

Nach der vielen Arbeit ist sie ganz fertig.
She's shattered after so much work.

FINDEN

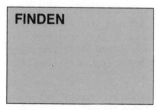

Das wird sich alles finden.

Everything will turn out all right.

Diese Situation scheint hoffnungslos zu sein, aber trotzdem bin ich überzeugt, daß sich alles finden wird.
This situation appears to be hopeless but I'm still convinced that everything will turn out all right.

GRAS

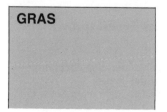

Darüber ist längst Gras gewachsen.

It's dead and buried. It's long forgotten. It's over and done with. It's a thing of the past.

Niemand spricht mehr von dem großen, politischen Skandal, der sich vor etlichen Jahren in unserer Stadt ereignete. Darüber ist längst Gras gewachsen.

No-one talks any more about the great political scandal that occurred some years ago in our city. It's a thing of the past.

Origin: **A term deriving from agricultural legal practice. If grass had grown over an area of land that had been damaged in some way, no claim could be made for the damage.**

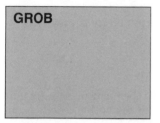

GROB

aus dem Gröbsten heraus sein

to see the light at the end of the tunnel, to be out of the woods

Monatelang lag mein Vater schwer krank im Krankenhaus, aber Gott sei Dank ist er jetzt aus dem Gröbsten heraus.
For months my father lay seriously ill in hospital, but thank God he is now out of the woods.

HANS

Was Hänschen nicht lernt, lernt Hans nimmermehr. (prov.)

You can't teach an old dog new tricks. (prov.)

Mit den neuen Lehrmethoden kommt jener grauhaarige Französischlehrer nicht zurecht. Was Hänschen nicht lernt, lernt Hans nimmermehr.
That grey-haired French teacher can't cope with the new teaching methods. You can't teach an old dog new tricks.

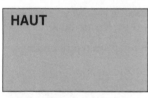

HAUT

mit heiler Haut davonkommen

to escape unhurt

Das Auto hatte Totalschaden, aber der Fahrer kam mit heiler Haut davon.
The car was a write-off but the driver escaped unhurt.

KATZE

Es ist alles für die Katz. (coll.)

It's all a waste of time.

Als ich eine kahle Stelle auf dem Kopf bemerkte, unterzog ich mich einer Haarwuchskur. Aber es war alles für die Katz — ich habe jetzt eine Glatze!
When I noticed a bald spot on my head I went for hair restoring treatment. However, it was all a waste of time — I'm now completely bald!

Origin: **From the proverb 'Was einer erspart mit dem Mund, das ist für die Katz' und den Hund!'**

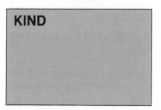

KIND

Gebranntes Kind scheut das Feuer. (prov.)

Once bitten, twice shy. (prov.)

Seit seinem Unfall fährt er nie wieder mit abgefahrenen Reifen. Gebranntes Kind scheut das Feuer.
Since his accident he'll never again drive with worn tyres. Once bitten, twice shy.

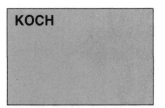

KOCH

Viele Köche verderben den Brei. (prov.)

Too many cooks spoil the broth. (prov.)

Wir können nicht alle zusammen dieses Zimmer tapezieren. Viele Köche verderben den Brei.
We can't all paper this room together. Too many cooks spoil the broth.

LACHEN

Wer zuletzt lacht, lacht am besten. (prov.)

He who laughs last, laughs longest. (prov.)

Klaus hat ·Christian damit ständig geneckt, daß er in der Schule zu fleißig arbeitete. In der Abschlußprüfung aber kam Christian durch, während Klaus erfolglos war. Wer zuletzt lacht, lacht am besten.
Klaus constantly teased Christian about working too hard in school. However, in the final examination Christian passed whilst Klaus failed. He who laughs last, laughs longest.

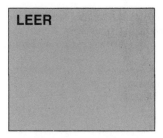

LEER

leer ausgehen

to go away empty-handed

Alle ihre Freundinnen haben beim Sportfest einen Preis erhalten, nur Ilse ist leer ausgegangen. Nächstes Jahr muß sie härter trainieren, um einen zu erreichen.
All her friends won a prize at the sports festival, only Ilse went away empty-handed. Next year she will have to train harder to get one.

LEHRGELD

Lehrgeld zahlen

to learn things the hard way

Leute, die nicht auf vernünftigen Rat hören wollen, müssen oft viel Lehrgeld zahlen.
People who don't like to listen to sound advice often have to learn things the hard way.

Origin: **The expression used to mean, quite simply, 'to pay for tuition'. In the extended sense the meaning is that certain kinds of experience, usually acquired with ease, have had to be acquired at the cost of some hardship to oneself, i.e. one has 'paid for' one's own tuition.**

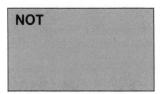

NOT

mit knapper Not davonkommen

to escape by the skin of one's teeth

Wir kamen mit knapper Not davon, als das Haus in Brand geriet.
We escaped by the skin of our teeth when the house caught fire.

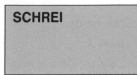

SCHREI

der letzte Schrei (coll.)
the in thing (coll.), all the rage (coll.)

Solche Frisuren sind jetzt der letzte Schrei.
Such hairstyles are now all the rage.

TAG

Man soll den Tag nicht vor dem Abend loben. (prov.)
There's many a slip 'twixt cup and lip. (prov.)

Ich hatte eben die Außenseite des Hauses frisch gestrichen und war mit mir sehr zufrieden, als ein plötzliches Gewitter meine Arbeit ruinierte. Man soll den Tag nicht vor dem Abend loben.
I had just freshly painted the outside of the house and was very pleased with myself when a sudden storm ruined my work. There's many a slip 'twixt cup and lip.

TÜR

einer Sache Tür und Tor öffnen
to open the floodgates to something

Wenn die Regierung in der bevorstehenden Lohnrunde der einen Arbeitergruppe eine Erhöhung über dem Acht-Prozent-Satz erlaubt, öffnet sie den Forderungen aller anderen Tür und Tor.
If the government allows one group of workers a rise above the eight per cent rate in the next pay round, it will be opening the floodgates to the demands of all the others.

37. RISKS

EI

jemanden wie ein rohes Ei behandeln
to handle someone with kid gloves

Du mußt sie wie ein rohes Ei behandeln. Sie ist sehr empfindlich.
You'll have to handle her with kid gloves. She's very sensitive.

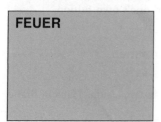

FEUER

mit dem Feuer spielen
to play with fire

Du willst die Armbanduhren nicht verzollen? Da spielst du mit dem Feuer — der Zollbeamte da drüben schaut dich mißtrauisch an.
You don't want to declare the watches? You're playing with fire — the customs officer over there is looking at you suspiciously.

KARTE

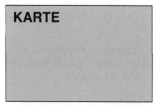

alles auf eine Karte setzen

to put all one's eggs in one basket

Setz nicht alles auf eine Karte. Bewirb dich um mehrere Stellen, nicht nur um diese eine.
Don't put all your eggs in one basket. Apply for several jobs, not just this one.

KOPF
LEBEN

Kopf und Kragen riskieren
sein Leben aufs Spiel setzen

to risk one's neck (coll.)

Der Feuerwehrmann riskierte Kopf und Kragen/setzte sein Leben aufs Spiel, um das kleine Mädchen aus dem brennenden Haus zu retten.
The fireman risked his neck to save the little girl from the burning house.

LÖWE

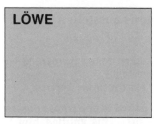

sich in die Höhle des Löwen begeben

to step into the lion's den

Siegfried hatte schwere Hemmungen gegenüber Mädchen, aber er begab sich in die Höhle des Löwen und bat eines um den nächsten Tanz.
Siegfried was very shy of girls but he stepped into the lion's den and asked someone for the next dance.

PULVERFASS

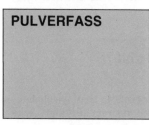

auf dem Pulverfaß sitzen

to be sitting on top of a volcano/on a powder keg

In das Land fahre ich nicht. Man sitzt dort auf dem Pulverfaß, weil Terroristenanschläge an der Tagesordnung sind.
I'm not travelling to that country. You're sitting on top of a volcano there because terrorist attacks are an everyday occurrence.

RÜCKSICHT

ohne Rücksicht auf Verluste (coll.)

regardless (of the consequences)

Im Fernsehinterview sprach die Sekretärin ohne Rücksicht auf Verluste von den dunklen Geschäften, die man im Finanzministerium trieb.
In the TV interview the secretary, regardless of the consequences, spoke about the shady dealings that were going on in the Ministry of Finance.

SICHER

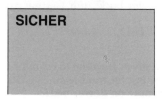

auf Nummer Sicher gehen (coll.)

to hedge one's bets, to play safe

Ich weiß nicht, ob ich nach Südtirol österreichische Schilling oder italienische Lire mitnehmen soll. Ich gehe auf Nummer Sicher und nehme beide Währungen mit.

I don't know if I should take Austrian schillings or Italian lire with me to South Tyrol. I'll play safe and take both currencies.

Origin: **'Nummer Sicher' is a humorous euphemism for 'prison'. Prisoners are kept safely (sicher) under lock and key in cells identified by a number (Nummer).**

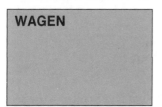
WAGEN

Wer wagt, gewinnt. (prov.)

Nothing ventured, nothing gained. (prov.)

Warum traust du dich nicht, Monika um eine Verabredung zu bitten? Wer wagt, gewinnt.
Why daren't you ask Monika for a date? Nothing ventured, nothing gained.

38. STUPITIDY, INCOMPETENCE

ARMUTSZEUGNIS

sich (dat.) ein Armutszeugnis ausstellen

to show oneself up, to make a fool of oneself

Durch seine dummen Bemerkungen in der Konferenz hat er sich ein Armutszeugnis ausgestellt.
He showed himself up by his silly remarks at the conference.

Origin: **A certificate of poverty issued to one whose possessions had been destroyed by fire. This entitled him to receive alms.**

**BEGRIFF
LEITUNG**

**schwer von Begriff sein
eine lange Leitung haben (coll.)**

to be slow on the uptake

Er ist wirklich schwer von Begriff./Er hat wirklich eine lange Leitung. Ich habe ihm schon dreimal erklärt, wie er dort hinkommt.
He is really slow on the uptake. I have already explained to him three times how to get there.

Origin: **Leitung: The imagery used here is taken from telecommunications, i.e. a long line.**

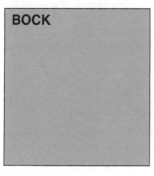
BOCK

den Bock zum Gärtner machen

to be asking for trouble

Die Helga kommt mit jungen Kindern nicht gut aus. Sie babysitten zu bitten, hieße ja den Bock zum Gärtner zu machen.
Helga doesn't get on with young children. To ask her to babysit is asking for trouble.

Origin: **The picture is of a goat given freedom to roam in a well tended garden. This is asking for trouble since goats will eat garden plants and trample on flower beds.**

BOHNENSTROH

dumm wie Bohnenstroh sein (coll.)

to be dense (coll.), *to be as thick as two short planks* (coll., Br.)

Richard ist dumm wie Bohnenstroh. Auch wenn ich ihm einen Einkaufszettel gebe, bringt er immer wieder die falschen Dinge nach Hause.
Richard is as thick as two short planks. Even when I give him a shopping list he keeps on bringing the wrong things home.

Origin: **From 'dumm wie ein Bund Stroh', 'Bohnenstroh' being a dialect development of 'Bund Stroh'. Straw was regarded as being of little value.**

DUMM

jemanden für dumm verkaufen (coll.)

to think someone stupid (coll.), *to take someone for an idiot* (coll.)

Für d a s verlangen Sie hundert Mark? Ich lasse mich von Ihnen doch nicht für dumm verkaufen.
You want a hundred marks for that? Don't take me for an idiot.

ELEFANT

sich wie ein Elefant im Porzellanladen benehmen
to behave like a bull in a china shop

Er versteht es nicht, taktvoll zu sein. Er benimmt sich wie ein Elefant im Porzellanladen.
He doesn't know how to be tactful. He behaves like a bull in a china shop.

FETTNÄPFCHEN

ins Fettnäpfchen treten (coll.)
to put one's foot in it (coll.)

Mit dieser dummen Bemerkung bin ich schön ins Fettnäpfchen getreten.
I really put my foot in it with that stupid remark.

Origin: **In many farmers' houses a bowl of fat (Fettnäpfchen) used to stand by the entrance door. When it rained or snowed, one would rub the fat into one's shoes as a means of protection for them. Whoever trod in the bowl accidentally, or tipped it over, would cause annoyance to the housewife because of the grease marks left in the entrance hall.**

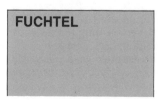

FUCHTEL

jemanden unter der Fuchtel haben (coll.)
to have someone under one's thumb (coll.)

Unsere Nachbarin hat ihren Mann wirklich unter der Fuchtel. Er wagt ohne ihre Erlaubnis nichts zu unternehmen.

Our neighbour really has her husband under her thumb. He daren't do anything without her permission.

Origin: **'Die Fuchtel' was a blunt broadsword used to administer heavy blows.**

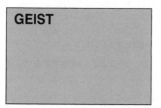

GEDÄCHTNIS

ein Gedächtnis wie ein Sieb haben (coll.)

to have a memory like a sieve (coll.)

Ich kann mich nie an seinen Geburtstag erinnern. Ich habe ein Gedächtnis wie ein Sieb.
I can never remember his birthday. I have a memory like a sieve.

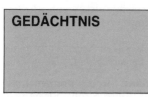

GEIST

von allen guten Geistern verlassen sein

to have taken leave of one's senses.

Bei diesem Wetter willst du eine Wanderung machen? Du bist wohl von allen guten Geistern verlassen.
You want to go on a hike in this weather? You've taken leave of your senses.

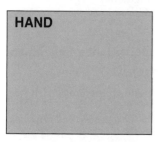

HAND

weder Hand noch Fuß haben

to make no sense at all

Deine Pläne, ein Geschäft zu gründen, haben weder Hand noch Fuß. Erstens hast du als Geschäftsmann zu wenig Erfahrung, zweitens leiht dir die Bank bestimmt kein Geld.
Your plans for setting up in business make no sense at all. First of all you have too little experience as a business man, secondly the bank is definitely not going to lend you any money.

KATER

einen Kater haben (coll.)

to have a hangover

Ich verstehe nie, warum deine Freunde immer noch so viel trinken, obwohl sie wissen, daß sie am nächsten Tag einen Kater haben.
I never understand why your friends still drink so much even though they know they will have a hangover next day.

Origin: **A contraction of 'Katzenjammer', previously called 'Kotzenjammer', meaning 'the misery of vomiting'.**

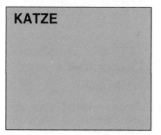

KATZE

die Katze aus dem Sack lassen

to let the cat out of the bag

Wir kauften ein neues Fahrrad für unsere Tochter zu ihrem Geburtstag. Aber es war keine Überraschung für sie — ihr Bruder hat vorher die Katze aus dem Sack gelassen.
We bought a new bicycle for our daughter on her birthday. However, it wasn't a surprise for her — her brother let the cat out of the bag beforehand.

LAPPEN

jemandem durch die Lappen gehen (coll.)

to slip through someone's fingers

Beinahe hatte ihn die Polizei erwischt, aber im letzten Moment ist er in ein Flugzeug eingestiegen und ihnen durch die Lappen gegangen.
The police had almost caught him but at the last minute he got into a plane and slipped through their fingers.

Origin: **From hunting. To contain the hunted game within the confines of the shoot, lines with long, coloured rags suspended from them were strung between trees. Most of the time the animals would shy away from these rags, but occasionally, in utter desperation, one would break through them.**

NASENSPITZE

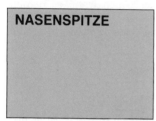

nicht weiter als seine Nasenspitze sehen (coll.)

to see no further than one's nose

Sie sieht nicht ein, daß wenn sie heute ihr ganzes Geld ausgibt, sie morgen keins haben wird. Sie sieht nicht weiter als ihre Nasenspitze.
She doesn't realise that if she spends all her money today she'll have none tomorrow. She can't see any further than her nose.

PANTOFFEL
PANTOFFELHELD

unter dem Pantoffel stehen (coll.)
ein Pantoffelheld sein (coll.)

to be henpecked (coll.)

Der arme Adalbert steht wirklich unter dem Pantoffel/ist wirklich ein Pantoffelheld. Er wollte gestern abend ins Kino gehen, aber seine Frau hat ihn gezwungen, die Küchendecke zu streichen.
Poor Adalbert is really henpecked. He wanted to go to the cinema last night but his wife made him paint the kitchen ceiling.

PFERD

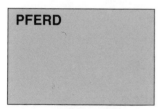

das Pferd beim Schwanz aufzäumen

to put the cart before the horse

Du sollst nicht das Pferd beim Schwanz aufzäumen. Mach zuerst deinen Führerschein und dann kauf dir ein Auto.
Don't put the cart before the horse. Pass your driving test first and then buy a car.

PULVER

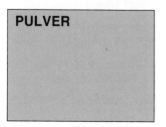

Er hat das Pulver nicht gerade erfunden.

He'll never set the world (or *Thames,* Br.) *on fire.* (coll.)
He's not a very bright spark. (coll.)

Mein Neffe bringt es im Leben bestimmt nicht weit. Er hat das Pulver nicht gerade erfunden.
My nephew's not going to get far in life. He'll never set the world on fire.

SCHNITZER

einen groben Schnitzer machen (coll.)

to make a real boob (coll., Br.)/*really blow it* (coll., Am.) *really muff it* (coll., Am.)

Ach, da habe ich einen groben Schnitzer gemacht! Ich habe die Ärmel dieses Kleids zusammengenäht!
Oh no, I've made a real boob (Am. I've really blown it) this time! I've sewn the sleeves of this dress together!

Origin: **If a wood carver makes a careless slip (einen groben Schnitzer) he can completely ruin a carving.**

SCHRAUBE
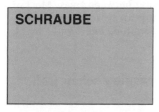

Bei jemandem ist eine Schraube locker. (coll.)

Someone has a screw loose. (coll.)

Bei ihm ist eine Schraube locker. Auch wenn es regnet, arbeitet er gern im Garten.
He's got a screw loose. Even when it's raining he likes to work in the garden.

THEATER

Es ist nur Theater. (coll.)

It's just play-acting. It's just put on. (coll.)

Schenk ihr keine Beachtung. Wenn sie so weint, ist es nur Theater.
Don't take any notice of her. When she cries like that it's just put on.

WERFEN
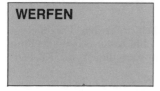

mit etwas um sich werfen

to bandy (coll.)/*chuck* (coll.) *something about*

Er ist ein großer Angeber. Er wirft immer mit hochgestochenen Wörtern um sich.
He's a great show-off. He always bandies big words about.

39. SUCCESS

ÄRMEL
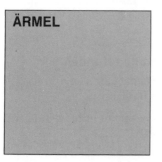

etwas aus dem Ärmel schütteln

to produce something just like that (coll.)

Unsere Kinder möchten eine Reise nach Disneyland in Florida machen, aber das Geld dafür können wir leider nicht aus dem Ärmel schütteln.
Our children would like to go to Disneyland in Florida, but unfortunately we can't produce the money just like that.

Origin: **The idea is of a conjuror producing something from up his sleeve.**

BOGEN
DREH

den Bogen heraushaben (coll.)
den Dreh heraushaben (coll.)

to have got the hang of something (coll.)

Lange fiel ihm die deutsche Wortstellung schwer aber nun endlich hat er den Bogen/Dreh heraus.
For a long time he found German word order difficult, but now at last he's got the hang of it.

Origin: **Bogen: From ice-skating. The ability to execute a turn (Bogen) suggested competence as a skater.**

DACH

etwas unter Dach und Fach bringen/haben

to get/have something in the bag (coll.), *to get/have something signed and sealed, to get/have something wrapped up* (coll.)

Bis Ende Juli hofft er, die Arbeit an seinem Buch unter Dach und Fach zu haben.
By the end of July he hopes to have the work on his book wrapped up.

Origin: **A building term. The essential parts of a house were at one time the roof (Dach) and the half-timbering (Fachwerk). Once these were erected the building was regarded as essentially complete, i.e. 'unter Dach und Fach'.**

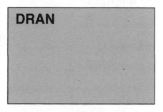

DRAN

gut dran sein (coll.)

to have a lot going for one (coll.), *to be well-off*

Christian ist wirklich gut dran. Er hat eine gute Frau, brave Kinder und ist im Beruf sehr zufrieden.
Christian really has a lot going for him. He has a good wife, nice children and is happy in his job.

EFFEFF
HANDGELENK

etwas aus dem Effeff können
etwas aus dem Handgelenk schütteln

to do something standing on one's head

Diese Arbeit ist unglaublich schwer, aber Herbert kann sie aus dem Effeff./schüttelt sie aus dem Handgelenk.
This work is incredibly difficult, but Herbert does it standing on his head.

Origin: **a) Effeff: From Roman civil law. The letter 'D', the abbreviation for the 'Digest' (the authoritative collection of laws), was written in such a way that it looked like a double 'f'. A lawyer who quoted regularly from the 'D' ('ff') was considered to be an expert. b) Handgelenk: The idea here is that something can be done so effortlessly that it can be done by the hand alone, without any help from the arm.**

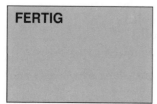

FERTIG

mit etwas fertig werden

to cope with something

Seit der Fusion der zwei Firmen haben wir im Sekretariat viel mehr Schreibarbeit. Wir werden aber damit fertig.
Since the merger of the two companies we've got a lot more paperwork in the office. We cope with it, though.

FLEISCH

jemandem in Fleisch und Blut übergehen

to become second nature to someone

Der junge Klavierspieler muß Tonleitern so oft üben, bis sie ihm in Fleisch und Blut übergehen.
The young pianist must practise scales until they become second nature to him.

GROSCHEN

Der Groschen ist gefallen. (coll.)

The penny has dropped. (coll.)

Lange verstand ich den Sinn dieses Gedichtes nicht, aber dann endlich ist der Groschen gefallen.
For a long time I couldn't understand the meaning of this poem but then finally the penny dropped.

Origin: **The picture is of a vending machine being set in operation when the inserted coin drops.**

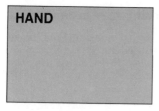

HAND

letzte Hand an etwas (acc.) legen

to put the finishing touches to something

Monatelang habe ich an meinem Segelboot gearbeitet, aber jetzt endlich lege ich letzte Hand daran.
For months I've been working on my sailing boat but now at last I'm putting the finishing touches to it.

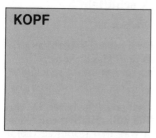

KOPF

seinen Kopf durchsetzen

to get one's own way

Klaus wollte ins Kino gehen, aber Renate wollte tanzen gehen. Klaus aber setzte seinen Kopf durch, und sie gingen beide ins Kino.
Klaus wanted to go to the cinema but Renate wanted to go dancing. However, Klaus got his own way and they both went to the cinema.

MACHEN

Das läßt sich schon machen. (coll.)

That can be done.

„Können wir an einem Tag Schloß Schönbrunn besichtigen und im Wienerwald spazieren gehen?"
„Ja, das läßt sich schon machen."
"Can we visit Schönbrunn Palace and go for a walk in the Vienna Woods in the same day?"
"Yes, that can be done."

PIKE

von der Pike auf dienen
von der Pike auf lernen

to work one's way up from the bottom
to learn something starting from the bottom

Der Polizeipräsident hat von der Pike auf gedient./hat seinen Beruf von der Pike auf gelernt. Er hat seinen jetzigen Rang durch hohe Dienstleistungen erworben.
The Chief of Police has worked his way up from the bottom./has learned his job starting from the bottom. He got the rank he now holds because of his good service.

Origin: **At one time the soldier with the pike represented the bottom rank in the military. It was from this rank that he had to work his way up.**

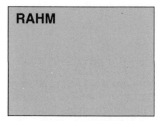

RAHM

den Rahm abschöpfen (coll.)

to skim off the cream

Jens hat die Firma gegründet und aufgebaut, aber sein Sohn hat den Rahm abgeschöpft, als er sie übernommen hat.
Jens founded the company and built it up, but his son skimmed off the cream when he took it over.

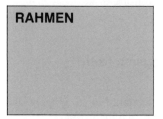

RAHMEN

aus dem Rahmen des Üblichen fallen

with a difference, out of the ordinary

Dieses Schulkonzert fiel völlig aus dem Rahmen des Üblichen. Das Orchester klang wie die Berliner Philharmoniker!
This was a school concert with a difference. The orchestra sounded like the Berlin Philharmonic!

RUNDE

über die Runden kommen

to pull through (coll.)

Am Anfang ihrer Ehe haben sie wegen geringen Einkommens große finanzielle Schwierigkeiten gehabt, aber sie sind über die Runden gekommen und haben nun keine Geldsorgen mehr.
When they were first married they had great financial difficulties because of their low income, but they pulled through and have no more money worries now.

seinen Kopf aus der Schlinge ziehen

to get out of a difficult situation, to get out of a tight corner (coll.)/*spot* (coll.)

In der Parlamentsdebatte konnte man den Minister nicht in die Enge treiben. Er verstand es meisterhaft, durch schlagfertige Antworten seinen Kopf aus der Schlinge zu ziehen.
In the parliamentary debate the Minister couldn't be cornered. He was brilliant at getting himself out of a difficult situation with quick-witted replies.

wie am Schnürchen gehen/laufen (coll.)

to go like clockwork

Unsere Schulreise nach Tirol mußten wir sorgfältig vorbereiten. Sie war ein Riesenerfolg, und alles ging/lief wie am Schnürchen.
We had to plan our school trip to Tyrol carefully. It was a huge success and everything went like clockwork.

Origin: 'Die Schnur' is the string from which a puppet is suspended and manipulated. Hence this idiom implies 'perfect control'.

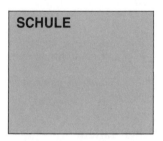

Schule machen

to become the accepted thing, to set a precedent

1971 wurde die britische Währung auf das Dezimalsystem umgestellt. Das hat Schule gemacht, und andere alte britische Maßsysteme werden jetzt allmählich abgeschafft.
In 1971 British currency changed over to the decimal system. That set a precedent and now other old British systems of measurement are gradually being abolished.

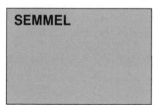

wie warme Semmeln weggehen (coll.)

to sell like hot cakes

Während der Hitzewelle im letzten Monat gingen die Kinderplanschbecken wie warme Semmeln weg.
During the heat-wave last month children's paddling pools sold like hot cakes.

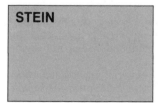

den Stein ins Rollen bringen (coll.)

to set the ball rolling (coll.)

Wenn du dein Auto verkaufen willst, mußt du den Stein ins Rollen bringen und ein Inserat in die Zeitung setzen.
If you want to sell your car you've got to set the ball rolling and put an advert in the paper.

VOGEL

den Vogel abschießen
to steal the show

Beim Hochzeitsmahl hat man viele gute Ansprachen gehalten, aber mit s e i n e r witzigen Rede hat der Eduard den Vogel abgeschossen. Wir sind vor Lachen fast geplatzt.
Many good speeches were made at the wedding reception, but Eduard stole the show with his witty speech. We almost split our sides laughing.

Origin: **From shooting. The term used when the best shot brought down the remains of the bird that had been the target in the competition.**

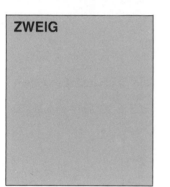

ZWEIG

auf keinen grünen Zweig kommen
to get nowhere (coll.)

Wenn er seinen Beruf nicht ernster nimmt, kommt er bestimmt auf keinen grünen Zweig.
If he doesn't take his work more seriously, he's sure to get nowhere.

Origin: **An old legal custom. On completion of the sale of a plot of land the former owner gave the purchaser a sod of earth containing a green twig, symbol of growth and prosperity. Anyone too poor to own land was never given a green twig.**

40. SURPRISE

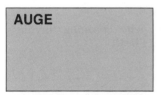

AUGE

große Augen machen
to be wide-eyed

Er machte große Augen, als er mein schönes, neues Auto sah.
He was wide-eyed when he saw my beautiful new car.

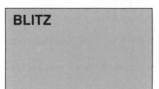

BLITZ

wie ein Blitz aus heiterem Himmel
like a bolt from the blue

Die Nachricht vom Tod seines Vaters kam wie ein Blitz aus heiterem Himmel.
The news of his father's death came like a bolt from the blue.

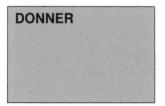

DONNER

wie vom Donner gerührt dastehen
to be thunderstruck

Als Brigitte erfuhr, daß sie in der Prüfung durchgefallen war, stand sie wie vom Donner gerührt da.
When Brigitte learned that she had failed the exam, she was thunderstruck.

KUHHAUT

Das geht auf keine Kuhhaut. (coll.)

It's absolutely incredible. (coll.)

Was der neue Abteilungsleiter von uns im Büro erwartet, das geht auf keine Kuhhaut.
What the new head of department expects of us at work is absolutely incredible.

Origin: **In the Middle Ages criminals were hauled to the place of execution on a cow's skin. Adulteresses were sewn inside a cow's skin and drowned in the nearest river or pond. Hence the idea that what would not go onto a cow's skin was worse than the worst crimes.**

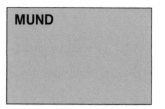

MUND

Mund und Nase aufsperren

to be open-mouthed

Als mein Opa ihr sagte, er wollte drachenfliegen gehen, sperrte meine Oma Mund und Nase auf.
When my grandad told her he wanted to go hang-gliding, my grandma was open-mouthed.

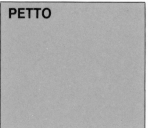

PETTO

etwas in petto haben

to have something up one's sleeve

Walter ist ein ausgezeichneter Redner. Er ist nie langweilig und hat immer etwas Lustiges in petto.
Walter is an excellent speaker. He is never boring and he always has something amusing up his sleeve.

Origin: **From the Italian 'in petto' meaning 'in one's breast', or figuratively, 'in one's heart'.**

ROT

etwas im Kalender rot anstreichen

to make a special note of something, to be a red-letter day

Er ist heute gut gelaunt? Das muß ich im Kalender rot anstreichen!
He's in a good mood today? I'll have to make a special note of that!

SAGEN

sage und schreibe

believe it or not

Sie ist eigentlich eine reiche Frau. Sie hat, sage und schreibe, mehr als zwei Millionen Mark auf der Bank.
She is actually a rich woman. Believe it or not, she has more than two million marks in the bank.

SPIESS

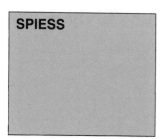

den Spieß umdrehen

to turn the tables

Seine Frau hat ihn beschuldigt, unnötig Geld für die Golfschläger ausgegeben zu haben, da hat er den Spieß umgedreht und auf ihren teuren Nerzmantel hingewiesen.
His wife accused him of spending money needlessly on the golf clubs, so he turned the tables and made reference to her expensive mink coat.

STAUB

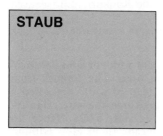

viel Staub aufwirbeln

to cause a great stir

Die Watergate-Affäre in den USA hat viel Staub aufgewirbelt.
The Watergate affair in the USA caused a great stir.

Origin: **The picture is of a passing carriage kicking up a lot of dust on the roadway.**

TAT

jemanden auf frischer Tat ertappen

to catch someone red-handed

Die Polizei ertappte den Einbrecher auf frischer Tat.
The police caught the burglar red-handed.

VERSCHLAGEN

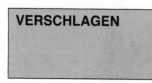

Etwas verschlägt mir die Sprache.

Words fail me. (coll.)

Dieses Hotel ist furchtbar. Es verschlägt mir die Sprache.
This hotel is dreadful. Words fail me.

WIMPER

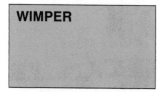

ohne mit der Wimper zu zucken

without batting an eyelid

Lotte sah die hohe Rechnung an, ohne mit der Wimper zu zucken.
Lotte looked at the expensive bill without batting an eyelid.

WUNDER

sein blaues Wunder erleben (coll.)

to get the shock of one's life

Willi erlebte sein blaues Wunder, als er sein Auto sah. Jemand hatte die Räder gestohlen!
Willi got the shock of his life when he saw his car. Someone had stolen the wheels!

Origin: **Derives from the blue haze conjurors used to prevent the audience from seeing clearly how the tricks were being performed.**

═ 41. THOROUGHNESS, COMPLETENESS, ═ ENTIRETY

BAUSCH

in Bausch und Bogen

lock, stock and barrel

Die große Elektronikfirma hat die Konkurrenz in Bausch und Bogen aufgekauft.
The large electronics company bought up its competitor lock, stock and barrel.

Origin: **To do with the purchase of a plot of land. 'Bausch' and 'Bogen' were demarcation lines. The former, from 'aufbauschen' = to billow out (e.g. of sail), suggested a gain for the purchaser in measured area; the latter, signifying an inward bending curve, suggested a loss. Hence, 'in Bausch und Bogen' came to mean 'all in all', 'without attention to detail'.**

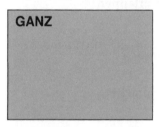

GANZ

aufs Ganze gehen

to go the whole hog (coll).

Um die Meisterschaft zu gewinnen, ging der Trainer aufs Ganze und kaufte zwei Spieler für mehrere Millionen Mark ein.
In order to win the championship the manager went the whole hog and bought two players for several million marks.

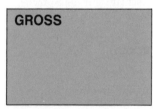

GROSS

im großen und ganzen

on the whole, by and large

Deine Arbeit ist im großen und ganzen gut. Nur solltest du ein bißchen mehr auf deine Schreibfehler achten.
Your work is good on the whole. You should take just a little more care over your spelling mistakes.

REGEL

nach allen Regeln der Kunst

thoroughly, by using every trick in the book (coll.)

Johann wollte mit uns nicht segelfliegen gehen, weil ihm leicht schwindlig wird, aber wir haben ihn nach allen Regeln der Kunst überredet, doch mitzukommen.
Johann didn't want to go gliding with us because he easily gets giddy, but by using every trick in the book we managed to persuade him.

Origin: **The Meistersinger, German musicians and poets of the 14th–16th centuries, had a statute-book ('die Tabulatur') in which were codified the laws of the art of singing (die Regeln der Kunst).**

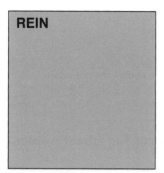

REIN

ins reine schreiben

to copy out neatly, to make a fair copy

Den Brief habe ich schon im Konzept geschrieben, jetzt muß ich ihn ins reine schreiben.
I've already written the letter in rough, now I've got to make a fair copy of it.

Origin: **'Die Reinschrift' means a fair copy, i.e. one without untidy crossings out. To write something 'ins reine', therefore, is to write it tidily so that it gives the impression of being 'clean', i.e. free of crossings out.**

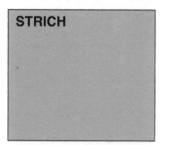

STRICH

nach Strich und Faden (coll.)

good and proper (coll.)

Als sein Vater erfahren hat, daß Wolfgang das Geld gestohlen hatte, hat er ihn nach Strich und Faden verprügelt.
When his father discovered that Wolfgang had stolen the money, he spanked him good and proper.

Origin: **From weaving, referring to the two directions of the thread (warp and woof).**

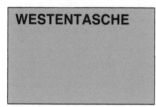

WESTENTASCHE

etwas wie seine Westentasche kennen

to know something like the back of one's hand

Georg kennt Hamburg wie seine Westentasche. Obgleich er gebürtiger Wiener ist, lebt er seit vielen Jahren dort.
Georg knows Hamburg like the back of his hand. Although he was born in Vienna, he has lived in Hamburg for many years.

42. TIME

HANDUMDREHEN

im Handumdrehen (coll.)

in the twinkling of an eye

Das Auto hatte eine Reifenpanne, aber im Handumdrehen hatte mein Vater den Reifen gewechselt.
The car had a puncture, but in the twinkling of an eye my father had changed the tyre.

**JUBELJAHR
ZEIT**

alle Jubeljahre (coll.)
alle heiligen Zeiten (coll.)

once in a blue moon (coll.)

Ich weiß nicht, wie es Gertrud geht. Ich sehe sie nur alle Jubeljahre/alle heiligen Zeiten.
I don't know how Gertrud is. I only see her once in a blue moon.

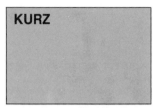

über kurz oder lang

sooner or later

„Du sollst nicht rauchen", sagte er seinem Sohn. „Über kurz oder lang wird es deiner Gesundheit schaden."
"You shouldn't smoke," he told his son. "Sooner or later it will damage your health."

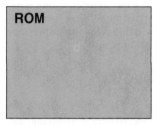

Rom ist auch nicht an einem Tag erbaut worden. (prov.)

Rome wasn't built in a day. (prov.)

Sei nicht entmutigt, daß du noch nicht perfekt Deutsch sprichst. Rom ist auch nicht an einem Tag erbaut worden.
Don't be discouraged that you don't yet speak·perfect German. Rome wasn't built in a day.

die Zeit totschlagen

to kill time

Mein Zug fährt erst in zwei Stunden ab. Um die Zeit totzuschlagen, lese ich mein Buch.
My train doesn't leave for another two hours. To kill time, I'll read my book.

die Zeit vertrödeln (coll.)

to fritter away time (coll.)

Kein Wunder, daß dein Brief nicht fertig ist. Du hast mit deinen Schallplatten unnötig viel Zeit vertrödelt.
It's no wonder that your letter isn't finished. You've frittered away a lot of time needlessly with your records.

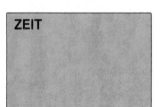

Kommt Zeit, kommt Rat. (prov.)

Time will tell.

Soll ich sie heiraten oder nicht? Die Entscheidung fällt mir schwer, aber kommt Zeit, kommt Rat.
Should I marry her or not? It's a difficult decision, but time will tell.

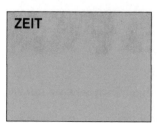

mit der Zeit gehen

to keep up with the times

Unser Geschäftsführer ist einer, der mit der Zeit geht. Er hat gerade das neueste Computermodell für sein Büro besorgt.
Our managing director is a person who keeps up with the times. He has just bought the latest computer model for his office.

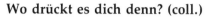

43. WORRY, ANXIETY

DRÜCKEN

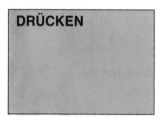

Wo drückt es dich denn? (coll.)

What's on your mind? What's troubling you?

Du siehst heute so traurig aus. Wo drückt es dich denn?
You look so sad today. What's troubling you?

Origin: **From 'Wo drückt dich der Schuh' (still used as the full form of the idiom above).**

FERTIGMACHEN

jemanden fertigmachen (coll.)

to get someone down (coll.)

Der ständige Lärm von der Straße macht mich fertig.
The constant noise from the street is getting me down.

HAAR

sich (dat.) keine grauen Haare über etwas (acc.) wachsen lassen

not to lose any sleep over something

Ich lasse mir über seine Fortschritte in Biologie keine grauen Haare wachsen. Er hat vorläufig Interesse daran verloren, aber das geht wieder vorbei.
I'm not losing any sleep over his progress in biology. He has temporarily lost interest in it, but it's just a phase he's going through.

HERZ

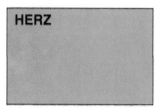

etwas auf dem Herzen haben

to have something on one's mind

Was ist denn, Udo? Mir scheint, du hast etwas auf dem Herzen. Sag mir einfach, was los ist.
What's up, Udo? It looks to me as if you've something on your mind. Tell me what's up.

KOHLE

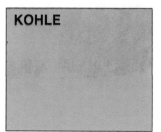

wie auf glühenden Kohlen sitzen

to be like a cat on hot bricks, to be on tenterhooks

Heute sitzt unser Sohn wie auf glühenden Kohlen, denn morgen erscheinen die Prüfungsresultate. Wenn sie für ihn nicht gut ausfallen, wird er nicht befördert.
Today our son is on tenterhooks because the exam results come out tomorrow. If they don't turn out well for him he won't get promotion.

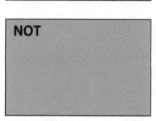

KOPFZERBRECHEN

jemandem Kopfzerbrechen machen

to be a headache to someone (coll.), *to be a worry to someone*

Das schlechte Benehmen ihres Sohnes macht den Eltern viel Kopfzerbrechen.
Their son's bad behaviour is a real worry to his parents.

NOT

seine liebe Not mit jemandem haben

to have one's hands full with someone

Wir haben mit dem jungen Gast unsere liebe Not. Er macht immer nur was er will und läßt sich nichts sagen.
We've got our hands full with our young guest. He always does what he wants and won't be told anything.

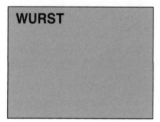

SCHAFFEN

jemandem viel zu schaffen machen

to cause someone a lot of trouble

Sein Auto macht ihm viel zu schaffen. Es ist ständig in Reparatur.
His car causes him a lot of trouble. It's constantly being repaired.

WURST

Es geht um die Wurst. (coll.)

It's do or die. (coll.) *It's the moment of truth. It's now or never.* (coll.)

Welche von den beiden Mannschaften heute das Spiel gewinnt, wird Meister. Jetzt geht es um die Wurst.
Whichever of the two teams wins the match today will be champions. It's do or die.

German Index

The German idioms and proverbs included in the book are listed here in alphabetical order of key words.
(Abbreviations: coll. = colloquial;   j-m = jemandem;   j-n = jemanden;   j-s = jemandes; prov. = proverb).

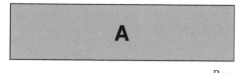

A

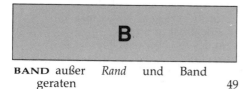

B

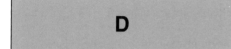
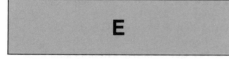

G

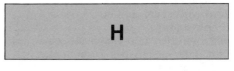

H

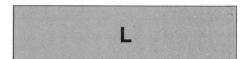

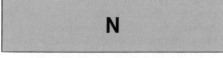

M

N

O

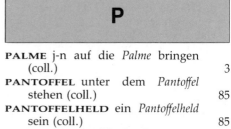

P

T

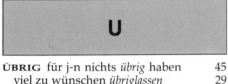

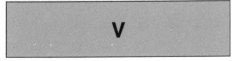

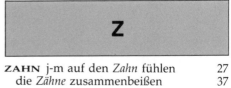

English Index

This index lists, in alphabetical order of key words, English idiomatic expressions which have a direct German idiomatic equivalent in this book. Also included in the list are common English sayings which have *no* direct German idiomatic equivalent. These are marked with an asterisk.

(Abbreviations: coll. = colloquial;   o.s. = oneself;   prov. = proverb;   s.o. = someone; s.t. = something)

A

Page

ACTIONS *Actions* speak louder than words (prov.)　7
ADVANTAGE to take *advantage* of s.o.　43
AIM to *aim* at someone　42
AIR to clear the *air*　26
　to pull s.t. out of thin *air*　64
ALARM a false *alarm*　30
ANGLE an inside *angle* on s.t.*
ARM to fling one's *arms* around s.o.'s neck　56
ASIDE as an *aside*　26

B

BACK to have broken the *back* of s.t. (coll.)　76
BAG to have/get s.t. in the *bag* (coll.)　87
BALANCE to be in the *balance*　67
BALL to be on the *ball* (coll.)　11
　to set the *ball* rolling (coll.)　90
BANDWAGON to jump on the *bandwagon**
BANDY to *bandy* s.t. about (coll.)　23, 86
BARGAIN to drive a hard *bargain* (coll.)*
BARREL to scrape the bottom of the *barrel* (coll.)*
BAT off one's own *bat* (coll.)　64
BED You've made your *bed*, now you must lie on it (coll.)　76

to be confined to *bed*　59
to have to stay in *bed*　59
to have got out of *bed* the wrong side (coll.)　1
BELIEVE *believe* it or not　92
BELL That rings a *bell* (coll.)*
BELT to tighten one's *belt*　72
BEND It's enough to drive you round the *bend* (coll.)　1
BESIDE to be *beside* o.s. with joy　48
BET to hedge one's *bets*　81
BEYOND in the back of *beyond* (coll.)　46
BIRD A *bird* in the hand is worth two in the bush (prov.)　74
　Birds of a feather flock together (prov.)　56
　to kill two *birds* with one stone (coll.)　74
BITE Once *bitten*, twice shy (prov.)　78
BLACK to be in *black* and white　69
BLAME to put the *blame* on s.o.　33
BLOOD to make s.o.'s *blood* boil (coll.)　3
BLOW to really *blow* it (coll., Am.)　86
BLUE like a bolt from the *blue*　91
BLUFF to call s.o.'s *bluff*　30
BONE to have a *bone* to pick with s.o.　18
　to make no *bones* about it　25
BOOB to make a real *boob* (coll., Br.)　86
BOOK to be in s.o.'s good *books*　55
BOOT The *boot* is on the other foot (coll.)*
BORE to *bore* s.o. to death　15
BOSOM to be *bosom* pals (coll.)　56
BOTTOM to learn s.t. starting from the *bottom*　89
　to work one's way up starting from the *bottom*　89
BREACH to step into the *breach*　61

C

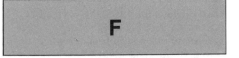

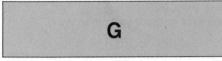

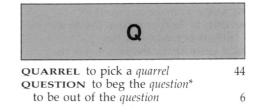

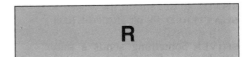

Y

LANGUAGE AND TRAVEL BOOKS
FROM PASSPORT BOOKS

Dictionaries
Vox Spanish and English Dictionaries
Harrap's Concise Spanish and English
  Dictionary
Harrap French and English Dictionaries
Klett German and English Dictionary
Harrap's Concise German and English
  Dictionary
Everyday American English Dictionary
Beginner's Dictionary of American
  English Usage
Diccionario Inglés
El Diccionario del Español Chicano
Diccionario Básico Norteamericano
British/American Language Dictionary
The French Businessmate
The German Businessmate
The Spanish Businessmate
Harrap's Slang Dictionary (French and English)
English Picture Dictionary
French Picture Dictionary
Spanish Picture Dictionary
German Picture Dictionary

References
Guide to Spanish Idioms
Guide to German Idioms
Guide to Correspondence in Spanish
Guide to Correspondence in French
Español para los Hispanos
Business Russian
Everyday Conversations in Russian
Everyday Japanese
Robin Hyman's Dictionary of Quotations

Verb References
Complete Handbook of Spanish Verbs
Spanish Verb Drills
French Verb Drills
German Verb Drills

Grammar References
Spanish Verbs and Essentials of Grammar
Nice 'n Easy Spanish Grammar
French Verbs and Essentials of Grammar
Nice 'n Easy French Grammar
German Verbs and Essentials of Grammar
Nice 'n Easy German Grammar
Essentials of Russian Grammar

Welcome Books
Welcome to Spain
Welcome to France
Welcome to Ancient Rome

**Just Listen 'n Learn Language
  Programs**
Complete language programs to learn
  Spanish, French, Italian, German and Greek.

Phrase Books
Just Enough Dutch
Just Enough French
Just Enough German
Just Enough Greek
Just Enough Italian
Just Enough Japanese
Just Enough Portuguese
Just Enough Scandinavian
Just Enough Serbo-Croat
Just Enough Spanish
Multilingual Phrase Book
International Traveler's Phrasebook

Language Game Books
Easy French Crossword Puzzles
Easy French Word Games and Puzzles
Easy Spanish Crossword Puzzles
Easy Spanish Word Games and Puzzles

Humor in Five Languages
The Insult Dictionary: How to Give 'Em
  Hell in 5 Nasty Languages
The Lover's Dictionary: How to Be
  Amorous in 5 Delectable Languages

Technical Dictionaries
Complete Multilingual Dictionary of
  Computer Terminology
Complete Multilingual Dictionary of
  Aviation and Aeronautical Terminology
Complete Multilingual Dictionary of
  Advertising, Marketing and Communications
Harrap's French and English
  Business Dictionary
Harrap's French and English
  Science Dictionary

Travel
Nagel's Encyclopedia Guides
World at Its Best Travel Series
Japan Today
Bon Voyage!
Hiking and Walking Guide to Europe

Getting Started Books
Introductory language books for Spanish,
  French, German and Italian.

PASSPORT BOOKS

Trade Imprint of National Textbook Company
4255 West Touhy Avenue
Lincolnwood, Illinois 60646-1975 U.S.A.